Let It Go
Workbook

ALSO BY T.D. JAKES

The T.D. Jakes Relationship Bible

64 Lessons for a Life Without Limits

Making Great Decisions

Reposition Yourself

Not Easily Broken

Can You Stand to Be Blessed?

Ten Commandments of Working in a Hostile Environment

He-Motions

Cover Girls

Follow the Star

God's Leading Lady

The Great Investment

The Lady, Her Lover, and Her Lord

Maximize the Moment

His Lady

So You Call Yourself a Man?

Woman, Thou Art Loosed!

Mama Made the Difference

Let It Go
Workbook

Finding Your Way to an Amazing
Future Through Forgiveness

T.D. Jakes

ATRIA PAPERBACK

New York   London   Toronto   Sydney   New Delhi

Contents

Welcome to Your Future!

Dear Friend,

I can hardly contain my excitement! I am so eager for you to work your way through this book because I know it can revolutionize your life. This workbook is so much more than words in ink on paper; it may very well be the key to a greater future than you've ever imagined for yourself. It's not simply a companion piece to my book *Let It Go*; it's an adventure waiting to happen, an exhilarating journey that will enable you to finally reach the potential you know is inside you and take you to a level of personal success you may have only dreamed of until now.

You may be thinking, "Wait a minute, Bishop Jakes. This is a workbook on forgiveness. It means I'm going to have to get in touch with a lot of the pain in my life and I'm going to have to process that pain and let it go. It may not be easy!"

You're right. Doing the work of forgiveness may not be easy and it will definitely take some time, but I promise you: It will be worth it. Sure, you will have to revisit some old wounds, some painful memories, and some situations or relationships that cut your heart to the quick. You'll have to unearth some feelings that may still be raw and raging. You may have to touch some emotional places that are still so tender you can hardly get near them, even if they resulted from something that happened long, long ago. I understand all of these realities; I'm sensitive to the challenge ahead of you. But forgiveness is a deliverer of destiny and a midwife of potential, so I still say: It's going to be worth the work!

Are you ready to make a life-changing investment in your personal healing, strength, and well-being? Are you ready to be relieved of the burdens of the past so you can throw your heart and your arms open to the amazing future that's available to you? Then let's get started. I'll be your coach and your cheerleader as you work through the pages ahead of you.

Looking forward to the realization of your potential and the fulfillment of your dreams,

Introduction: Why Forgive?

Before you begin: Please familiarize yourself with the Introduction to Let It Go, *pages 1–16.*

At least two truths apply as you begin this workbook. The first is that you didn't just emerge on the scene of your life as the person you are today. All kinds of factors and experiences have shaped who you are. Hopefully, some of those influences have been good and positive. Most likely, as is true for everyone, some of them have been painful and negative.

The second truth is that you don't have to stay where you are. You can change; you can grow; you can become your very best self and you can thrive as you live the life you are destined to live.

Because of the difficult circumstances you've encountered and the wounds your soul has sustained, your life may not yet be everything you long for it to be. This is why forgiveness is not just important, it's essential. As you embrace the process of forgiving those who have hurt or offended you, your heart begins to heal. As healing comes, you grow stronger, wiser, and better able to reach your potential for future success and happiness.

What Is Forgiveness, Anyway?

Sometimes the best way to describe what something is, is to start by defining what it *isn't*. I think this is especially true about forgiveness because it is so often misunderstood and misinterpreted. Before we go any further, let's correct some of the common misconceptions of forgiveness.

- Forgiveness is *not* overlooking, ignoring, or denying a hurt or an offense, and it does not require your anger to disappear.

- Forgiveness is *not* excusing damaging or wrong behavior.

- Forgiveness does *not* rob you of personal power or exonerate the person who hurt you.

- Forgiveness does *not* trivialize your trauma or lessen the pain you have experienced.

- Forgiveness is *not* forgetting the hurtful or harmful things people have done or pretending those things never happened.

- Forgiveness does *not* mean you should restore trust in someone who hurt you or that you should have an ongoing relationship with that person.

So, what is forgiveness?

- Forgiveness is the force that liberates you from your past and sets you free to embrace your future.

- Forgiveness unburdens your soul of agonies that could infect every area of your life for the rest of your life.

- Forgiveness relieves that emotional ache you cannot seem to escape, the one that holds you back when you try to move forward and weighs you down when you try to rise up.

- Forgiveness takes a realistic assessment of the damage done to your soul, accepts that, and takes deliberate steps toward healing.

- Forgiveness is what will release you to a new level of purpose, vision, creativity, vitality, intimacy with others, and success in every area of your life.

- Forgiveness is essential if you are going to grow into the fullness of the person God created you to be—and it is indispensable to fulfilling your destiny.

- Forgiveness is one of the best gifts you can ever give yourself.

1 Looking at the list of things forgiveness is *not,* check the ones that have held you back from extending forgiveness to someone.

_____ I thought forgiveness meant I had to overlook, ignore, or deny a hurt or an offense.

_____ I thought forgiveness meant I had to excuse damaging or wrong behavior.

_____ I thought forgiveness would exonerate the person who hurt me.

_____ I thought forgiveness would trivialize the trauma or lessen the pain I have experienced.

_____ I thought forgiveness meant I had to try to forget the hurtful or harmful things people have done to me or to pretend those things never happened.

_____ I thought forgiveness meant I had to restore trust in someone who hurt me or that I had to stay in some kind of relationship with that person.

2 What is the most powerful and liberating truth about forgiveness you have learned in this section of the book?

_____

_____

_____

_____

Remember: "It will be more than worth the effort to free yourself from a burden that's been crippling you for far too long" (*Let It Go*, p. 4).

Identify Your "Ouch!"

Success is always intentional. It doesn't just happen, but I believe you are destined for it if you'll make an effort to achieve it. So let's identify some of the issues that are holding you back from being the person you are meant to be so you can begin to break free from them and move into a new and wonderful dimension of success in your life.

1 A question I ask in *Let It Go* is "How did you get to this point in your life?" Since a variety of factors have shaped the person you are today, let's focus on some of them. I'll ask you to make some notes about how some specific circumstances have made you who you are. Be sure to include both positive and negative factors. We need to deal with it all in order to make progress.

- **Your Birth:** Were you wanted when you were conceived and born? Did your physical life come into being as a result of trauma or as a result of love? Did your parents welcome your arrival in the world, or were you viewed as a burden in some way?

  _____

  _____

  _____

  _____

- **Your Growing Up:** Did you feel surrounded by love and support as you were growing up, or did you lack the nurture and guidance you desperately needed? Did you have good friendships and family relationships, or were you exposed to harmful people? Were you prepared for adulthood, or did you have to figure things out on your own?

  _____

  _____

_____

_____

_____

- **Your Hurts and Wounds:** What are the most significant sources of pain in your life and how have those things influenced the person you have become?

_____

_____

_____

_____

- **Your Social Life:** As an adult, how have your friendships and romantic relationships affected you? Has your heart been hurt? Have you been blessed with good people in your life? Perhaps some of both. Record your thoughts below.

_____

_____

_____

_____

_____

_____

- **Your Family Life:** A family can be the greatest institution on earth or a place of great pain and heartache; sometimes it's a combination of both. How has your family experience shaped who you are today?

_____

_____

_____

_____

_____

- **Your Work Life:** How have things that have happened along your career path or in your workplace affected the person you are right now?

_____

_____

_____

_____

_____

_____

- **Your View of the Future:** How does the way you think about the future affect who you are and how you feel about your life today? If it's not so great, don't worry; I believe it will change by the time you finish this book.

_____

_____

_____

_____

_____

_____

2 Look back at your answers in the previous section. Which of those things are still painful to you? List them below because there's a good chance these may be areas or situations in which forgiveness can set you free.

_____

_____

_____

_____

_____

_____

3 Circle the common but unfortunate experiences that have shaped who you are today.

Abandonment	An accident	Anger
Being devalued	Being fired	Being lied about
Being lied to	Being used	Betrayal
Broken trust	Deceit	Disappointment
Disrespect	Divorce	Emotional abuse

Exposure to violence	Failure	Fear
Feeling overlooked	Guilt	Having something stolen
Illness	Injustice	Loss of any kind
Not being cared for	Physical abuse	Poverty or lack
Regret	Rejection	Sexual abuse
Shame	Trauma	Verbal abuse

Other:

_____

_____

Remember: "There's nothing wrong with you that cannot be changed" *(Let It Go,* p. 12).

End the Masquerade

Once we begin to identify some of the situations that have wounded our souls, we become responsible for doing something about them. If we don't, an infection of the heart begins to grow and affect every area of our lives.

1 Can you see how the wounds of your past can affect the following areas of your life? Check all that apply to you:

_____ your marriage or romantic relationships

_____ your relationships at work

_____ your relationships with your children

_____ your relationships with your parents or siblings

_____ your ability to engage in community or civic activities

_____ your job performance

_____ your ability to maintain a clean, orderly home or workspace

_____ your ability to trust other people

_____ your willingness to make new friends

_____ your appetite and eating habits

_____ your motivation to take care of yourself

_____ the way you dress or carry yourself

_____ your emotional health and well-being

_____ your spending and financial management

_____ your perspective on your potential or abilities

_____ your willingness to take risks or try new things

_____ your view of the future

Are you surprised by how many you checked? The good news is this: Everything the hurts of your past have affected negatively can change. Learning to work through the wounds you've suffered and forgive the offenders can influence every single one of these situations in a positive way!

2 Take one or two of the items you checked above and jot down a few sentences about how you would like to see your current situation change as healing and freedom begin to happen in your life.

_____

_____

_____

_____

_____

_____

_____

_____

_____

_____

_____

_____

_____

Remember: "As we let go of the debris, the emotional detritus that has clogged our valves and prevented our functioning at full capacity, we will rediscover ourselves, our best selves, and at that point, all those around us will reap the reward" *(Let It Go,* p. 14).

Write It Off

I believe the ability to forgive is directly connected to the fulfillment of potential in a person's life. That means you. Write, draw, paste photos, or otherwise express your answers to these questions: Who would you be if there were absolutely no limits on your life? What would you do, how would you feel, what kind of character would you have, what goals would you pursue, what risks would you take if you were to be serious about becoming the best possible you?

Let It Go

Workbook

Chapter 1
Giants and Dwarfs

Before you begin: Please familiarize yourself with Chapter 1 of Let It Go, *pages 17–34.*

A big idea is within your reach right now, this very moment. It can bring peace to your troubled heart; it can heal a broken relationship; it can raise the level of joy you experience in life. And it might lower your blood pressure! In so many ways, this big idea can change your life and can even change the world around you. You know what it is: forgiveness.

One reason forgiveness is a big idea is that it releases you into a large expanse of possibilities, opportunities, vision, and destiny. Small ideas don't do such powerful things. Small ideas keep you cramped and limited; they keep you focused on what *is* and what *was* instead of on what *can be;* they lock you into the past and the present instead of launching you into the future. Small ideas trap you in a small life. I don't think you want that, so let's explore some ways the big idea of forgiveness can catapult you into greater success and enjoyment than you ever thought possible.

1 In your own words, why is forgiveness a big idea?

_____

_____

_____

_____

_____

2 Think about a past or present situation in which you need to find the grace to forgive. Describe what could happen if you embrace a small idea such as revenge or trying to get even with someone versus what could happen if you embrace the big idea of forgiveness.

- Your situation:

  _____

  _____

- Potential results of a small idea:

  _____

  _____

- Potential results of a big idea:

  _____

  _____

- Which results would you rather live with—those of the big idea or the small?

  _____

  _____

Remember: "Most people who harbor animosity in their hearts against others do so because they remain on the reservation of what has happened in the past rather than escape to the much larger idea of a better future" (see *Let It Go,* p. 22).

Chickens and Eagles

You don't have to be a bird expert to know there are huge differences between chickens and eagles. Chickens cluck around on the ground; they eat little kernels of corn or grain and they don't often go beyond the barnyard or their own limited environment.

Eagles, on the other hand, are born to soar. These majestic animals seem to own the skies; they are made for high places. They don't settle for eating morsels of grain; they are capable of getting fresh meat.

You can deal with the things that have hurt you with a chicken's mind-set or from an eagle's perspective. You can keep your eyes focused on the ground in front of you and never escape the confines of your current environment. Or you can cast your vision toward the sky like an eagle, as high as you can go. You can accept what happens and decide that it will not limit you or hold you down. As you act on that decision, you'll set yourself free to dream your best dreams and live your best life.

1 On the scale below, from 1 to 10, where are you currently in your ability to handle the wounds and offenses that result from interactions with other people?

1. Chicken ······ **2** ······ **3** ······ **4** ······ **5** ······ **6** ······ **7** ······ **8** ······ **9** ······ **10. Eagle**

2 Think about a specific situation in which you have been hurt, disappointed, or treated unfairly. What deliberate steps can you take as you respond to these circumstances to transition yourself from chicken-like thinking to an eagle attitude?

_____

_____

_____

_____

_____

Remember: "Your mission—should you accept it—is to look up and consider who you are and where you're going" (*Let It Go*, p. 25).

Catch It Early

We often see the warning signs of trouble in business deals, personal relationships, and social situations, but we ignore or dismiss them. This can be fatal, because letting these things fester can be like a cancer in your soul.

You can't rely on blood work or imaging to tell you if an emotional cancer is growing inside you. You have to have the personal awareness, sensitivity, and discernment to diagnose it yourself. When we can identify and catch illnesses of the heart early, before they take root and spread throughout our personalities, our chances are best for avoiding trouble and being able to resolve problems.

Remember: "We have to set aside time to really communicate what's going on inside us and discover what's really going on inside the other person if we want to foster an atmosphere of health, well-being, and intimacy" *(Let It Go,* p. 30).

1 Look back and describe a situation in which you now realize you overlooked or totally failed to recognize the danger signs. What were the warnings you didn't see or didn't heed?

---

2 What were the consequences of a faulty "early detection system"? How might things have turned out differently had you identified and corrected problems sooner?

_____

_____

_____

_____

_____

3 You do not have to repeat the cycle of the past. You can have a fresh start right now. Think about your current relationships. Are there any warning signs that you need to pay attention to? What are they?

_____

_____

_____

_____

_____

Remember: "I have seen, time and time again, frustration imitate cancer and silently engulf people who avoid confrontation to the point of becoming martyrs simply because they lack the courage or the skills to be forthcoming about little areas of discontentment and resentment" *(Let It Go,* pp. 30–31).

You Have to Give It to Get It

There's no escaping an ancient principle about forgiveness: If you want it for yourself, you have to extend it to others.

Everyone needs forgiveness. People who've hurt and offended you need it and you need it from the people you've wounded or wronged. It takes a person with a really big mind and a really big heart to admit their own shortcomings and to say, "I have failed So-and-So, and I need to be forgiven." But this is a powerful and necessary step in the big-idea process of forgiveness.

1 Is there anyone you feel holds a grudge against you and you wish would forgive you? Who is it and what are the circumstances?

_____

_____

_____

_____

_____

_____

2 As you think about your own need for forgiveness, ask yourself where you have failed to forgive someone else. That may be the reason for the "blockage" you sense right now. Whom do you need to forgive and why would that have the power to release the forgiveness you need?

_____

_____

_____

_____

_____

_____

Remember: "In order to forgive others, we must be willing to look at our own ability to hurt, offend, and injure those around us, often the people we love most" *(Let It Go,* p. 32).

Write It Off

Using words, pictures, or any creative method you'd like, express what choosing the big idea of forgiveness could mean for your life or for your destiny.

Chapter 2
Offenses Do Come

Before you begin: Please familiarize yourself with Chapter 2 of Let It Go, *pages 35–53.*

While many of us would prefer to live our lives without conflict, pain, or disappointment, the truth is that *it's not going to happen.* Anytime human beings are involved in any kind of situation, we will find differences in opinions, differences in priorities or values, differences in work ethics or communication styles. So many differences can contribute to great strength in an organization or a family, but they can also lead to significant conflict.

One lesson we must learn is that many relationships get off to a good start. If they didn't begin on a positive note, we wouldn't stay in them. They only sour later on, and when they do, we regret some of the early investments we made, secrets we shared, or trust we placed in others.

Wise people acknowledge the fact that conflict is inevitable. They don't fear it. They can hope it won't happen, but they realize that it probably will. When it does they don't let it send them into an emotional tailspin; they plan for it so they will not be devastated when it takes place.

1 Check the situations in which you've had a relationship that started off positively and become negative later on.

_____ your business or professional life

_____ your neighborhood or building

_____ your church or religious community

_____ your immediate family

_____ your extended family and/or your spouse's family

_____ your children's friends or parents of their friends

_____ your civic or social activities or clubs

_____ your gym or recreational endeavors

_____ your work on a committee

_____ your dealings with a vendor or service provider

2 Think about the situations you checked in question 1 and choose one to focus on. Had you known it would go south, what would you have done ahead of time to prepare to handle the conflict effectively?

_____

_____

_____

_____

_____

_____

_____

_____

3 Think about a situation you are currently involved in that seems to be going well. What can you do now to prepare yourself to deal successfully with conflict or trouble when it arises, as it inevitably will?

_____

_____

_____

_____

_____

_____

_____

Remember: "Wise people plan in advance the terms of resolution while hoping they will never need to use them" *(Let It Go, p. 37)*.

The Golden Age of Television

Many of us learned about life, conflict, and relationships from Hollywood scriptwriters who created 30-minute scenarios about imaginary people with imaginary lives.

We learned about conflict and resolution from Fat Albert and his friends, Aunt Bee and Andy, the Bradys, the Waltons, and so many others.

Perhaps the lessons we learned from television that hurt us most were these: 1) Conflict can arise and be resolved in 30 minutes; and 2) Next time the show comes on, everyone involved will have completely forgotten the conflict and moved on. The truth is: Problems take time to work out effectively, and conflicts can influence relationships for weeks, months, and years into the future.

1 Take a trip down memory lane. What three television shows do you think most influenced your view of life and relationships?

---

2 Based on what you learned from television shows, what did you come to believe
about relationships and the trouble that can arise in them?

_____

_____

_____

_____

_____

3 What do you wish you had learned about people and relationships as a young
person that you didn't learn? What insights have you gained the hard way, and
what advice would you now give the young people in your life?

_____

_____

_____

_____

_____

Remember: "Life does not reflect a scripted entertainment segment but is instead often filled with complex issues, conflicted people, and complicated situations that cannot be easily resolved before the next commercial break" (*Let It Go*, pp. 37–38).

Great Expectations

At some point, we all have to discover what real life and real relationships are all about. We must realize that, often, various influences including but certainly not limited to televisions shows have skewed our perspectives on things. We have to acknowledge that we built a set of expectations about people and about how life should be on a faulty foundation; we need to put aside those expectations, build a foundation of truth, and construct new, reasonable expectations that align with the basic realities of life and relationships.

1 Below is a list of ten common expectations that don't always materialize in relationships. Check the ones that apply to you:

_____ I have expected conflict to be fairly easy to manage if I took the steps to confront it.

_____ I have expected people to appreciate the fact that I was willing to confront and resolve conflict.

_____ I have expected people to respect my desire to openly communicate my feelings of disappointment or offense.

_____ I have expected to be able to articulate my perspective to other people and have them start to see things my way.

_____ I have expected other people to want to resolve conflict in the same way I wanted to resolve it.

_____ I have expected other people to understand why I was hurt or offended once I explained it.

_____ I have expected conflicts to be resolved quickly.

_____ I have expected to be able to resolve a conflict, then go on as if it never happened.

_____ I have expected to be able to maintain my opinions and point of view, not to have to entertain other people's perspective and admit that they may be right.

_____ I have expected to receive forgiveness at the end of conflict resolution, but not to have to extend forgiveness to someone else.

2 Take a look at the statements you checked above. For each one, use the space below to write a sentence or two that revises each expectation to make it more realistic. For example, if you expected confrontation to be easy once you chose to confront it, your revised expectation might be something like this: "I have learned that working through conflict takes time, effort, patience, and willingness to consider viewpoints other than my own."

_____

_____

_____

_____

_____

_____

_____

_____

_____

_____

_____

_____

_____

Remember: "If we haven't stopped to question what we've learned and consider how it's working for us, then we set ourselves up for repeated failure" *(Let It Go,* pp. 38–39).

This Is Not That

We can get into trouble when we fail to understand and differentiate what's personal from what's professional. The two areas are different, and need to be kept separate.

While it's important to be pleasant and cordial in your work relationships, it's also important to know where to draw the line. Everyone in your life does not need to be allowed into your inner circle, and understanding where the boundaries are—and the potential danger of violating them—can greatly reduce the possibility of misunderstanding, offense, hurts, or betrayal in your life.

1 Below are several sets of two possible scenarios. One is appropriate or acceptable in the context of your job, the other should be reserved for personal relationships. In the blanks provided, put a "W" for the one that applies to a work setting and a "P" for the one that belongs in a more personal context.

_____ a brief, friendly comment about a person's nice-looking outfit or accessory

_____ a long discussion about what to wear on your date next weekend

_____ mentioning the fact that a family member is hospitalized

_____ going into detail about a family member's illness, addiction, or other problems

_____ making one statement about how much you appreciate getting a paycheck

_____ worrying aloud about your debt and how you are going to pay all your bills

_____ acknowledging that you worked late last night to finish an assignment

_____ going into detail about drama with your teenager, which meant you had to stay up late to finish an assignment

_____ mentioning the fact that you need to watch what you eat

_____ talking about how you are an emotional eater and sharing details about how you have so many personal problems that you just can't seem to control your eating right now

_____ inquiring about the general well-being of someone's family or spouse

_____ asking for specific details about a situation with a person's spouse or family member

2 Have you ever been directly or indirectly affected by a situation in which a personal relationship or a business relationship suffered because the people involved could not separate the two? What happened? What personal boundaries were missing? How did the fact that people were personal friends damage their business relationship?

_____

_____

_____

_____

_____

_____

_____

_____

_____

_____

3 Think about a good, positive, potential-filled professional relationship you have right now. How can you begin right now to put appropriate boundaries around that situation?

_____

_____

_____

_____

_____

_____

Remember: "When you handle your coworkers like personal friends you open yourself up for the possibility of offense" *(Let It Go,* p. 39).

Get a Handle on It

One of the best reasons to learn to handle conflict well is that the way you handle it is not only crucial to your well-being, it's also inseparable from life's promotions and your destiny. Most promotions come wrapped in a package of conflict, in some way. Every time a person gets promoted to greater influence, authority, responsibility, or visibility, the potential for conflict rises right along with those new opportunities.

Often, what separates strong, healthy people from those who still have a lot of growing to do is their ability to handle conflict—the same thing that separates those who are ready for promotions in life from those who aren't.

1 Here's a list of common ways people handle hurts and offenses. Which ones apply to you?

_____ anger and/or frustration

_____ judgment

_____ rejection

_____ stonewalling/silent treatment

_____ icy stares

_____ withdrawal

_____ bursting into tears

_____ emotional outbursts

_____ blowing things out of proportion

_____ denial

_____ making a big deal of minor issues, while ignoring the major issues

_____ adopting a victim mentality

_____ making threats

_____ trying to hurt the other person as much as he or she hurt you

_____ giving in to the other person because of fear or intimidation

2 The list below includes the opposite responses of those above. Check the top three responses you'd like to develop when someone does you wrong. Over time, you can develop them all, but start with just three that are reasonable for you.

_____ patience

_____ willingness to explore the other person's perspective

_____ understanding there's a problem but you are not personally rejected

_____ willingness to have a calm, open conversation about the offense

_____ neutral or positive body language

_____ staying in the situation even when it's uncomfortable

_____ not breaking down in tears, but taking a deep breath

_____ holding your tongue instead of spouting off words you'll regret

_____ seeing things clearly and interpreting them accurately

_____ accepting the fact that there's a problem and facing it head on

_____ focusing on the major problems, not the picky little issues

_____ seeing yourself as a human being worthy of being treated well

_____ not resorting to empty threats

_____ seeking resolution, not revenge

_____ standing up for yourself in a wise and healthy way

3 What specific steps can you take to develop the responses you checked in question 2?

_____

_____

_____

_____

_____

_____

_____

Remember: "Every promotion brings each of us into a higher level of exposure to conflict. If you can't handle the pressure, you can't function in the promise that is inherent to that level of promotion" *(Let It Go,* p. 41).

Curing "People Phobia"

When someone has wounded, offended, or betrayed you, especially if it happens repeatedly, if the wounds are particularly painful, or if you are a very sensitive, giving, creative, or sincere person, you may become a bit skittish of people. You may decide that people cannot be trusted or will always hurt you, and conclude that the best way to live your life is to keep others at a distance. To fill the void, you may turn to some type of creative or intellectual endeavor or some other activity that allows only minimal interaction with others. This may be nice for a while, but over the long term it's not healthy emotionally or socially. What's really happening is that you are becoming more committed to the offense and its ramifications in your life than you are to moving forward. Your past becomes more important than your future. I urge you not to let this happen. People can definitely cause pain, but we still need them in our lives.

1 Has a situation with another person damaged you to the point that you avoid meaningful relationships? Instead of investing in people, what have you given your time and energy to? Circle all that apply to you.

Art	Beauty or appearance	Career
Children's activities	Computers	Crafts
Exercise	Good nutrition	Hobbies
Home repair	Junk food	Pets
Politics	Redecorating	Social Causes
Sports	Study or learning	Taking classes
Travel	TV or movies	Volunteering

2 Think about two of the greatest people you know well. What qualities make them great and why do you feel safe in a relationship with them?

_____

_____

_____

_____

_____

_____

_____

_____

_____

_____

_____

3 What qualities would you like to develop in yourself so other people will feel safe when they're in a relationship with you?

_____

_____

_____

_____

_____

_____

Remember: "Because you were born to love and born to give, not doing so can affect every area of your life." *(Let It Go,* p. 44).

Write It Off

Think about an offense or a difficult or unfair situation you are going through right now. Dream just a little bit and write about the good things that could potentially arise from it.

Chapter 3
Where Did This Come From?

Before you begin: Please familiarize yourself with Chapter 3 of Let It Go, *pages 55–71.*

Feelings and responses that are deeply embedded in us are part of our basic human "wiring." They're the reactions that come naturally to us, our "default settings." You know what I mean: Some people scream and flail and throw fits over the most minor offense, while others seem to weather serious conflicts, betrayals, or disappointments with complete composure and grace.

Often in a relationship, you can accurately predict how someone will respond in a situation because you're familiar with his or her default settings. You have your default settings too. You may have identified some of them in the previous chapter when you checked some of the ways you respond when hurt or offended.

You may or may not realize that your default settings influence the way you feel about forgiveness. They may lead you to forgive quickly or they may make you reluctant to do so. If you're wired to forgive easily, terrific! If not, you can learn to reset your defaults so you can break free from the unforgiveness that will prevent you from moving forward into your destiny and your future.

1 I've listed below some reasons people have a hard time forgiving. Check all that apply to you.

_____ I feel that the situation delayed, damaged, or robbed me of the future I envisioned for myself. Because of the situation, my hopes and dreams now seem impossible.

_____ I don't believe the offender has sufficiently apologized or atoned for the situation.

_____ I don't want to forgive because I want to protect myself from further hurt.

_____ I feel that I was deceived in the situation and it brought shame or embarrassment to me in front of other people.

_____ I believe my trust was violated in this situation.

_____ I can see that the situation has resulted in lost opportunities for me.

_____ Because of the situation, my soul has silently suffered abuse, rejection, and neglect.

2 People's default settings influence how easily they forgive (or not) and the degree to which they allow emotions to be in control. Why is it important for you to control your emotions instead of allowing them to control you?

_____

_____

_____

_____

_____

_____

Remember: "Anytime you are being controlled by your emotions rather than you controlling them, you are a prisoner without a jail cell" *(Let It Go,* p. 58).

It's All Relative

The people who raise us set powerful emotional examples for us. Sometimes they don't know they're teaching us their coping mechanisms or relational strategies, and sometimes we don't realize how much we've adopted their habits as our own until someone points out the fact that we seem to have the same default settings as our parents, caregivers, and/or siblings.

The default settings in your emotional makeup—emotional pathologies such as rage, bitterness, jealousy, and the refusal to forgive—come from the people you were around most during your formative years. If you can recognize the harmful predispositions your soul has inherited, you can correct them and thereby position yourself for enormous success in the future.

1 Think of two people who raised you or cared for you and therefore influenced you tremendously. Use the space below to describe how each of these people chose to deal with being wronged or wounded.

_____

_____

_____

_____

_____

_____

_____

2 As you think about how your caregivers handled conflict, emotional pain, or offense, what similarities do you see between how they dealt with these kinds of situations and how you deal with them?

_____

_____

_____

_____

_____

_____

_____

_____

3 What kind of example are you setting for your children or other young people? What lessons are they learning about forgiveness and handling offenses from you? If you don't like the lessons you think you're teaching, what steps will you take to change them?

_____

_____

_____

_____

_____

_____

_____

Remember: "Most families have a pathology that has been passed down from generation to generation" (*Let It Go,* p. 61).

Don't Drink the Passed-Down Poison

Many families tell stories about people who did them wrong or about someone who betrayed Uncle So-and-So. Those who hear these tales usually perpetuate the family's negative opinion of the offender. These accounts of wounding and wrongdoing are much more than dinner-table conversation; they can actually promote prejudice, resentment, or even hatred toward individuals, races, genders, or organizations. Retelling the stories and stirring up bad feelings from long ago is like passing a cup of poison around the picnic table at a family reunion and seeing everybody take a sip. Focusing on past wounds fosters generational unforgiveness, which puts future generations in the same emotional bondages their relatives have endured; it deters their destinies, just as it did for their mothers' and fathers'; and it keeps them bound to the bitterness of the past instead of being able to savor the sweetness of the future.

1 Think about an offense or a negative situation in your family's past. Which words describe your family's general attitude toward it?

_____ acceptance

_____ anger

_____ attempts to interpret the story fairly, trying to see all perspectives

_____ bitterness

_____ compassion

_____ demands for justice

_____ desire for revenge

_____ forgiveness

_____ indignation

_____ hatred

_____ jealousy

_____ justifying someone's actions

_____ mercy

_____ refusal to hold a grudge

_____ resentment

_____ pity toward the victim

_____ praying for the offender

_____ prejudice

_____ pride

_____ understanding

_____ unforgiveness

2
Generally speaking, your family holds unforgiveness or negative bias toward people associated with a certain (check all that apply):

_____ age group

_____ business or industry affiliation

_____ educational achievement/lack of achievement

_____ gender

_____ geographic region

_____ neighborhood or part of town

_____ race

_____ religious affiliation

_____ socioeconomic category

_____ school, college, or university

_____ sports team

_____ physical appearance

_____ political party

3 If you have negative opinions or bitterness toward anyone associated with categories you checked above, look at each one and ask yourself if you have been personally offended or whether your offense has been passed down to you through your family. List the ones that have hurt you personally and then list the ones you hold a grudge against because of your family or caregivers.

_____

_____

_____

_____

_____

Remember: "What one individual did to your grandmother is not cause for you to avoid an entire gender, race, or church denomination of the same kind!" *(Let It Go,* p. 63).

Unlearning Learned Behaviors

We can only learn to become stronger and healthier in handling our emotions and dealing with other people if we unlearn the lessons that led us to the way we've behaved all of our lives.

One way we untangle ourselves from faulty coping mechanisms and relational strategies is to reduce the influence of people who keep us stuck in the past. I'm not suggesting cutting off relationships; I'm simply encouraging you to minimize negative influences and surround yourself with people who will help you deal with things more successfully, not hold you in the patterns of your past.

1 Think about the people you are drawn to or have been around for years. Do they hold grudges or speak negatively about those who have hurt them? Do they fly off the handle anytime the slightest offense happens? How would you describe these people emotionally?

_____

_____

_____

_____

_____

_____

2 If you are surrounded by people who aren't good influences on you, then it's time to move on and get involved with more mature people who handle life better. What qualities would you like to see in the people who are close to you?

_____

_____

_____

_____

_____

_____

Remember: "If we allow ourselves to remain stuck, then we will only end up with others who are also immobilized, all while those with full tanks and well-tuned engines accelerate toward their goals" *(Let It Go,* p. 68).

Living by the Law of the Jungle

Every area of life is its own type of "jungle." Every arena has rules, often unspoken, that those who live in it must understand and obey, not only to thrive, but also to survive!

You are not living in the same context in which your parents or grandparents existed. The attitudes that enabled them to endure the environments in which they lived need to be updated and revised to empower you to deal effectively with the realities of your life today.

When you enter a new jungle in your life, you must adapt to the culture there. This definitely applies to the way you handle your emotions and relate to other people. As you advance into your future, new environments will require you to adapt to new standards of thinking and behavior. I know it may stretch you, but it'll be good for you!

1 What are some of the jungles you live in now that you didn't live in before?

_____ marriage

_____ parenthood

_____ work environment after being in school or staying home to raise children

_____ new levels of influence, authority, or responsibility

_____ corporate leadership

_____ financial responsibility

_____ divorce and dealing with an ex

_____ caring for aging parents

_____ living in a new city or neighborhood

_____ entering into a faith community or civic organization

2 Look at the items you checked in question 1. For each, make a note about the new rules you're having to learn and abide by.

_____

_____

_____

_____

_____

_____

_____

_____

_____

_____

Remember: "If we don't learn how to respond and express our disagreement without becoming vitriolic and retaliatory, we will regress back into the old jungle whose laws we imitate and lose the precious gift" *(Let It Go,* p. 70).

Sever a Root from the Family Tree

As we bring this chapter to a close, we've hopefully uncovered many of the reasons you respond the way you do in certain situations. The most important point I want to make is this: You can escape the training and influences of your past and become the person you were meant to be!

1 What one influence or learned behavior from your family do you think has the most potential to sabotage your present and your future?

_____

_____

_____

_____

2 Look at your answer to question 1. What is the opposite of it? For example, if you said, "holding grudges," the opposite would be something like, "refusing to hold things against people when they have sincerely apologized." What deliberate steps can you take today to cut off the influence of this negative quality in your life and cultivate its opposite?

_____

_____

_____

_____

_____

_____

Remember: "Today as you purpose in your heart that you don't want to respond to your present out of the pain of your past, you are one step closer to stepping into your future with newfound freedom" *(Let It Go,* pp. 70-71).

Write It Off

I invite you to take a few moments to write or express in some other creative way whatever comes to you about your family's influence over your current behaviors, especially your behavior in difficult situations and under circumstances where forgiveness is called for—and about how you can change it!

Chapter 4
Silence Doesn't Mean Consent

Before you begin: Please familiarize yourself with Chapter 4 of Let It Go, *pages 73–89.*

Anyone who has ever been wounded by an angry verbal explosion or a whispered threat knows that words can be devastating. But I submit to you that words that *aren't* spoken can be far more damaging than words that are spoken. What we fail to express to others often hurts us—and others—more than what we do communicate.

Many people can remember a time when they or someone else allowed frustration, disappointment, misunderstanding, or resentment to simmer like unsavory soup on the back burner of a stove instead of speaking up. The difference is that simmering makes a soup taste better, while it makes a relationship taste bitter!

It's not always easy or comfortable to mention little things before they become big things, but learning to do so will enable you to avoid emotional explosions and relational meltdowns.

1 Think about one person in your personal or professional life. When something is bothering him or her, does that person display any of the signs below? Know that some of these things are habits for certain people and do not indicate anything is wrong. Look for things that are out of the ordinary for this person and check all that apply.

_____ becoming quiet

_____ withdrawing

_____ claiming to be too busy for you when that's obviously not true

_____ getting a certain look in the eye

_____ twisting a piece of hair or tapping fingers on a desk

_____ changing work habits or lowering standards

_____ sighing dramatically and repeatedly

_____ acting distracted when you try to communicate

_____ seeming to be in a hurry or becoming impatient

_____ being late when you've agreed to meet or being late to work

_____ changing the subject when you ask if there's a problem

_____ denying that anything is wrong when you ask

_____ spending excessive time on the computer or watching TV

_____ avoiding you

_____ acting annoyed with you, but not telling you why

_____ not participating as usual in meetings

_____ a change in tone of voice, so you know the person is annoyed

_____ not interacting as usual with coworkers

_____ having a mess in a usually neat office

_____ not attending nonmandatory work events

_____ taking an unusually high number of sick days

_____ becoming short-tempered

2 Have you ever had someone blow up at you before you even knew there was a problem? Describe the situation.

_____

_____

_____

_____

_____

_____

_____

_____

_____

_____

_____

3 Many people have a story about attempting to manage their own intense emotions until they reached a breaking point. Have you ever surprised someone else by losing your temper when that person didn't know anything was wrong? Describe the situation.

_____

_____

_____

_____

_____

_____

_____

_____

_____

_____

Remember: "If we don't learn to communicate honestly and transparently, the silent frustration of our unmet expectations will poison us with their toxicity and no one else knows" *(Let It Go,* p. 73).

How Much Can You Handle?

In order to maintain proper relationships with others, we need to know a little bit about them. This means that we have to spend time with them and really get to know them. A relationship of any kind will require maintenance, and I say there is proactive power in preventative maintenance. It *takes* time, but it never *wastes* time.

In *Let It Go,* I mention that I believe the preventative maintenance is so important that I don't take on more friendships than I can handle. That's a lesson I've had to learn over the years, but it's proven to be wise and good both for my friends and for me. I would encourage you to think about making a similar decision and see if it seems right to you.

There's a difference between relationships that need *preventative* maintenance (and they all do) and relationships that are *high* maintenance. When people in your life become too high maintenance, you may end up with simmering resentments and frustrations.

Being able to handle relationships means being willing to do the preventative maintenance on them as you go along—talking about the little things that bother you *when they start* to bother you, noticing when something doesn't seem right about the other person, and forgiving minor misunderstandings and offenses as they happen, not letting them simmer for days, weeks, months, or even years.

1 Let's face it. Some people require a lot more attention than others. Which three relationships in your life are the most high maintenance?

_____

_____

_____

_____

2 Which three relationships in your life require the level of maintenance that's comfortable for you?

_____

_____

_____

_____

3 Think about your life and your responsibilities. How many relationships do you honestly think you can maintain well and who are the people with whom you can maintain them?

_____

_____

_____

_____

Remember: "Don't take on more than you are willing to take care of. Count the cost of the relational investment and commit to the necessary maintenance before you lose the opportunity to know the other person" *(Let It Go,* p. 75).

What Do You Do?

You may have a one-on-one relationship or "one-on-many" relationship (such as a consultant with a business organization, a coach with a team, or pastor with a congregation). You may also be part of a group or team that has relationships with other groups or teams.

Regardless of the situation, you're not in a relationship alone. This means that you not only need to identify the early warning signs of trouble in yourself and in others, you also need to know what to do about them.

In *Let It Go,* I tell the story of a couple who ignored the little signals of anger and disappointment in their marriage until it reached a breaking point. Maybe you can relate to their story because of something that has happened in your marriage, in a friendship, or with a work associate or supervisor. Perhaps you totally understand how things intensified to a dangerous level because you've handled your own problems with the same silence this couple employed or you've had someone's long-brewing anger erupt all over you when you didn't even know that person was unhappy.

We have to learn to be honest with ourselves and honest with each other. It's a process that takes time and willingness from both people, but it's worth the effort.

1 Think through the significant relationships in your life. You may need to use a journal or a separate sheet of paper for this exercise. Ask yourself the following questions about each one:

- How do I *really* feel about this relationship? Do I feel safe in it? Am I happy in it? Is anything at all bothering me about the other person or the relationship?

- How is the communication in this relationship? Do we have a history of not understanding each other? Or do we have a history of open, honest dialogue?

- Am I seeing any warning signs of trouble in the other person? Does this person have a pattern of acting like things are fine, then blowing up before I even knew there was a problem?

- When was our last disagreement? What was it about? Did we resolve it completely? Did the other person and I agree that the matter was over? Do I feel deep inside that the other person may still have questions or complaints about it? Do I have any lingering questions or complaints about it?

- When was the last time this person and I cleared the air? Did I sense that everything that needed to be said was said?

2 The point of this chapter is that things can *seem* fine in a relationship, but be very bad under the surface. That's why it's so hard. Here are some suggested

questions you can put in your own words and ask people as you try to discern what's happening inside them and keep your relationship healthy. Suggestion: Ask some questions that require more than a one-word, "yes" or "no" answer!

- "Remember when we had that disagreement about (specify the topic)? Do we need to talk about it again?"

- "A few minutes ago, when you got a little upset over what I did (specify the action), what was going on? Why was that a problem?"

- "I'm getting the impression you're not happy with what I just said. What was wrong with it?"

- "You know that conversation we had this morning about (specify the topic)? What else do you want to say about that?"

- "I can tell you are not happy about what I just did (or said). Shoot straight with me: What is it that you don't like?"

Remember: "Understand that forgiveness isn't just needed when a violation occurs. It is also needed when intimacy is denied, needs aren't met, or honest communication has waned" (*Let It Go*, p. 78).

Outlove the Offense

There are times in life when people love so much, give so much, and suffer so much that they end up with what I call "donor fatigue." They've spent all the emotional resources they have; they end up depleted, and the relationships involved often come to an end.

There are other times in which one person's love for another trumps an offense, when love is strong enough to push through any kind of pain and keep loving anyway. If we can identify why we give too much and understand how to outlove an offense, there's an excellent chance we can salvage our own well-being and our relationships.

1 Have you ever suffered from donor fatigue? Describe that situation.

_____

_____

_____

_____

_____

_____

_____

_____

_____

_____

_____

2 I've listed below ten common reasons people give more than they have and end up depleted. What personal qualities do you have that got you to the point of giving too much? Check all that apply.

_____ compassionate

_____ eager to help

_____ lacking good personal boundaries

_____ merciful

_____ overly respectful

_____ wanting to please people

_____ wanting to be liked or accepted

_____ wanting my talents or skills to be recognized

_____ wanting to be included

_____ unable to say no

Other:

_____

_____

3 Are you in a situation in which you can choose to outlove an offense you're struggling with right now? As you think about that, consider these questions and circle yes or no:

- Do I really want to outlove the offense?

Yes   No

- Do I have the personal resources (time, energy, support, wisdom) to do so?

Yes   No

- Do both parties agree that this relationship is worth saving?

Yes   No

4 If you answered yes to the three questions above, what practical steps can you take as you endeavor to outlove the offense?

_____

_____

_____

_____

_____

_____

Remember: "The toll of constant withdrawals with no deposits leaves the [personal and relational] equity depleted and the balance plummets until the bottom line shrinks to zero" *(Let It Go,* p. 81).

Sub-Mission

Every relationship has some kind of mission. Marriages have a mission and so do friendships. Work relationships that involve high or medium levels of interaction have a mission, as do casual professional relationships involving outside advisors or vendors. In every arena, when two parties can put the misdeeds of the past behind them and submit to the mission of the future, great things can happen!

1 If you are in a specific situation where relational restoration needs to happen, it's important to define the mission to which you and the other party need to submit. What is the mission?

_____

_____

_____

_____

_____

_____

2 Think about your professional life. Are you submitted to the mission of your company? How can you engage better and support that mission more effectively?

_____

_____

_____

_____

_____

_____

_____

Remember: "[Submitting to the mission] means that we agree that the 'we' of the relationship is more important than the 'me' of it. And both of us are willing to submit to the mission of 'us'" *(Let It Go, p. 82).*

Put the Lessons to Work

If you really are committed to enjoying restored relationships now and better relationships in the future, you'll have to implement the insights you've read in this chapter of this workbook and in Chapter 4 of *Let It Go*. In that chapter, I listed eight practical steps to avoid the damaging impact of silence and to develop more effective communication. You can refresh your memory by looking at them on pages 87–88 of *Let It Go*, and I encourage you to do that now.

1 Which of these steps offer you a chance to change your mind? For example, did you once believe that when someone didn't like something you did, it meant they didn't like you? Now you know that's not true!

_____

_____

_____

_____

_____

2 Look at your answer to question 1. What new thoughts and beliefs do you need to develop in order to avoid the damage silence can do to a relationship?

_____

_____

_____

_____

_____

3 How will you practice the new thoughts you need to think in order to become a better communicator?

_____

_____

_____

_____

_____

_____

Remember: "My prayer has become: 'Lord, teach us how to say what we mean even when it risks making one another temporarily uncomfortable'" *(Let It Go,* p. 84).

Write It Off

Write—or express in some other creative way—what you would say to someone with whom you currently have silent conflict if you knew for sure that there would be no negative repercussions. This will get you in touch with how you *really* feel.

Chapter 5
The Power of a Pure Heart

Before you begin: Please familiarize yourself with Chapter 5 of Let It Go, *pages 91–107.*

Unforgiven offenses and unresolved anger create blockages in the heart of who you are, the core of your being, your inner self. These blockages are just as threatening to your emotional health as problems in your biological heart are to your physical well-being.

To be a strong, vibrant, healthy person ready to embrace the great future that lies before you, you must find ways to remove that blockage so that life, peace, happiness, and success can energize you and flow through you.

1 What is the offense, disappointment, or betrayal that you are still angry about, the one you just can't seem to get past?

_____

_____

_____

_____

_____

_____

_____

2 Can you see how holding on to the situation you described in question 1 could be damaging to your emotional health? Describe the negative impact this situation continues to have on you.

_____

_____

_____

_____

_____

_____

_____

_____

_____

_____

_____

Remember: "People who free themselves from long-term emotional debilitation find themselves more blessed, more productive, and much more grounded than those who become blocked by incidents, tragedies, and injustices" *(Let It Go,* p. 92).

Offenses Create Clogs

Anytime you suffer a wound or an offense, you can relive it, rehearse it in your mind, and let it fester in your soul; or you can let it go in a healthy way. If you hold on to it, it becomes like plaque in your arteries, creating a blockage that will impede the vitality you would otherwise enjoy. If too many soul-wounds and offenses build up, they'll create blockages that may lead to an emotional cardiac arrest—a moment of genuine crisis.

Letting things go is often easier said than done, but people who step up to the challenge keep their souls unpolluted and uncluttered, free to live, learn and laugh. They also keep their inner beings in position to embrace and enjoy the future instead of using the heavy chains of unforgiveness to lock their hearts into the past.

1 The process of unclogging your emotional arteries often begins by accepting the fact that you are stuck in a situation. You may be replaying what happened over and over in your mind, unable to solve it resolve it, yet unable to break free from its painful impact. Think about the place where you're stuck. In what ways is it keeping you from moving forward?

_____

_____

_____

_____

_____

_____

_____

_____

_____

_____

2 Is it possible that you're stuck because you've been waiting for someone else to make the first move—perhaps, to apologize? Circle yes or no.

Yes   No

3 If you circled yes to question 2, let me encourage you to stop waiting. Take responsibility for your own emotions and for your own freedom and destiny. Will you choose right now to pursue forgiveness (not necessarily a restored relationship) in your own heart? Circle yes or no.

Yes   No

Remember: "If blockage of your physical heart is potentially lethal, so, too, is the clutter than can contaminate the valves and ventricles of your inner heart" (*Let It Go,* pp. 91–92).

Courage and Wisdom: A Winning Combination

Many times, we can find the courage to confront a situation (and sometimes that's because we are so angry), but finding the wisdom to know how to resolve issues and move forward *after* a confrontation can be a challenge.

1 In the space provided, describe what courage means to you and how you are going to be courageous as you move forward in forgiveness.

_____

_____

_____

_____

_____

_____

_____

2 In the space provided, describe what wisdom means to you and how you are going to be wise as you move forward in forgiveness.

_____

_____

_____

_____

_____

_____

Remember: "Lingering issues left without resolution can become lethal to your well-being and block the blessings of creativity, opportunity, and openness to new experiences." *(Let It Go,* p. 92).

Anger Can Be an Asset

In some cultures, families, and organizations, anger is not viewed as a healthy or positive emotion. The fact that anger often gets a bad rap is unfortunate because the truth is that anger is a normal human response. If left on its own, it can grow, fester, and become quite dangerous. But, if focused and handled appropriately, it can be extremely helpful and constructive.

Consider my "top ten list" of anger's best qualities, qualities that only exist when anger is managed well:

1. Anger can provide focus, energy, and determination.

2. Anger is a clear sign that you care about someone or something (even yourself!).

3. Anger calls attention to the wrongs that threaten your well-being.

4. Anger will help you confront and correct what you might otherwise ignore to your own detriment.

5. Anger can help you find your way to restoration and peace.

6. Anger forces people to give their perspective on the truth.

7. Anger lets others know when they have violated our boundaries.

8. Anger releases energy and motivates us to do something about a matter we might have allowed to fester.

9. Anger gives us courage to do what needs to be done.

10. Anger acknowledges the wounds and offenses we have suffered, takes us to a point of catharsis surrounding those things, and enables us to enter into the future without the baggage of the past.

1 Generally speaking, and using the top ten list in this section as a guide, are your
  typical displays of anger positive and constructive or negative and destructive?

1. Destructive ····· **2** ···· **3** ····· **4** ····· **5** ····· **6** ····· **7** ····· **8** ····· **9** ····· **10. Constructive**

2 Think about someone who you think handles anger well. How does that person
  manage his or her temper? What lessons can you learn from this person about
managing your anger in a more positive way?

_____

_____

_____

_____

_____

_____

_____

_____

_____

_____

Remember: "Anger is a God-given emotion that if managed correctly can be
of huge benefit" *(Let It Go,* p. 95).

Own Your Anger

If we want to be mature individuals, we must take responsibility for the way we feel. We must express our feelings in healthy ways and learn to deal with conflict for ourselves, not expecting anyone else to do it for us. And when we find ourselves angry, we must own our anger and handle it appropriately.

Owning your anger means admitting it, asking yourself why you were angry, working to resolve that situation, and making amends as best you can toward the person who sustained your rage. It also means keeping your anger positive instead of negative. One sure way to know when constructive anger begins to give way to destructive anger is that it jumps the tracks of reason, clear thinking, and sound judgment. Anger becomes negative when it sits and seethes in the soul for too long or when it causes you to do things that are out of character for you or dangerous to other people.

Feeling anger is part of being human. Make sure you take responsibility for your anger and handle it a positive, constructive way.

1 Have you ever completely lost your temper in a situation? Did you (check one):

_____ ignore it and pretend it didn't happen or wasn't a big deal?

_____ justify it and defend yourself?

_____ apologize halfheartedly and go on?

_____ apologize sincerely, begin to look for the root cause of your anger, explain the situation as best you could without being defensive, and commit to do better next time?

2 Look at your answer to question 1. If you checked one of the first three options, as you think about the situation now, how could you have owned and handled your anger better?

_____

_____

_____

_____

3 Is there a situation in your life that you have been angry about for quite some time? It's time to take steps to own it and resolve it before it becomes more dangerous. What one action can you take today to own your anger and move toward resolution? It can be simple—maybe as simple as letting yourself feel the anger and pounding your fist on a pillow!

_____

_____

_____

_____

4 Think of a specific situation and write one example of how you could express anger in a destructive way and one example of how you could express it constructively.

_____

_____

_____

_____

_____

_____

_____

_____

_____

_____

Remember: "Own your anger and stop being in denial" *(Let It Go,* p. 96).

Passing the Stress Test

Medically speaking, one purpose of a stress test is to identify blockages that could have a negative impact on the health of your heart. When a blockage is present, it must be removed. Doctors know exactly how to do this; they know much better how to eliminate physical blockages than most of us know how to get rid of our emotional blockages!

One of the first ways to remove something that has you clogged emotionally is to look for the lessons in it and the positive potential it holds. Perhaps a situation infuriated you, but it also helped you learn how to stand up for yourself. Perhaps you blew your top and damaged a relationship so badly that you finally learned how to handle your anger better. Maybe someone violated you so severely that you have now become an effective advocate for others who suffer in the same way.

When you have mined the gold of an ugly situation by taking what is valuable from it, then it's time to let it go for good. You have transformed something that could have destroyed you into a tool that has made you strong, beautiful, and immensely valuable to those around you.

1 Think about a situation that made you angry. What are two lessons you learned from it?

_____

_____

_____

_____

_____

2 Think again about the same situation you used to answer question 1. How did going through that situation make you stronger, and how can you encourage or strengthen others as a result of what you endured?

_____

_____

_____

_____

_____

_____

_____

_____

_____

_____

Remember: "Even the most hideous of events in our lives have something to teach us, some purpose through which we can learn, be wiser, and grow stronger" *(Let It Go,* p. 102).

Relieving the Energy Crunch

If you've ever been *really* hurt or *terribly* offended or *deeply* disappointed—and I suspect you have—then you know that such soul traumas live on in your memory long after they are finished in reality. This is harmful for several reasons, but I want to highlight two of them right now.

First, replaying an incident in your mind tends to emphasize and reinforce the emotional pain you feel. Second, reliving a bad situation, even if you only relive it in your head, takes a lot of energy! You see, it's almost impossible to think and think about something difficult or wrong without feeling the pain again on some level. Pain leads to anger, and anger takes energy.

As long as you rehearse everything that happened, you will not only stay chained to the past in your thinking, you will give away your energy to dream about and plan for your future.

1 Do you ever find yourself tired after a day when you've thought a lot about a past offense or disappointment? Circle yes or no.

Yes   No

If you circled yes, it's understandable. All that thinking takes a lot of energy!

2 Here's a simple question, but your answer should give you great insight. Has all your rehearsing, reliving, and replaying that negative, hurtful situation helped you put the situation behind you and move forward? Circle yes or no.

Yes   No

Remember: "When anger diverts your energy away from where it should be going, you fail to discover your highest and best use of your gifts" (*Let It Go*, p. 104).

Heart Surgery

To get your heart pure after an offense, you do the things we've discussed thus far. To help *keep* your heart pure, you can do things like replacing toxic friends with supportive, healthy ones. You can reduce the level of disappointment with people by learning to pray and strengthen your spiritual life instead of expecting people to give you more than they have to offer. Your options are plentiful!

I am excited about your future, so let me ask the questions from the book again and give you a space to answer them.

1 What "arterial relocation" have you done to refresh the damaged areas of your life? Have you exited a bad relationship and entered into a healthy one? Have you decided to seek affirmation and comfort from God instead of other people? Have you made and acted on some decisions to manage your anger more effectively?

_____

_____

_____

_____

_____

_____

2 The process of maintaining a pure heart never ends; it's ongoing. What have you learned in this chapter that will help you unclog your heart more quickly and easily next time anger and unforgiveness try to lodge there?

_____

_____

_____

_____

_____

_____

Remember: "I am encouraging you through prayer, counseling, or beating a pillow to find a way to unblock your heart and move forward in your life" *(Let It Go,* p. 107).

Write It Off

Today I invite you to dream. Dream about who you could become and what you would do with your life if you were not wasting one single bit of energy rehearsing past offenses, reliving angry situations, or bemoaning past disappointments. Write down, draw, or express your impressions in a creative way of your choosing.

Chapter 6
Write It Off

Before you begin: Please familiarize yourself with Chapter 6 of Let It Go, *pages 109–119.*

I n *Let It Go,* I tell the story of a credit union that wrote off a debt for me after I was downsized. If this has ever happened to you, then you know the relief I felt! I had paid my debt diligently during the time I was employed, but when my job was eliminated, I simply couldn't pay the bill anymore. I didn't have the resources to do so.

This story teaches a great lesson about life and forgiveness: In many situations, there comes a time when it's in everyone's best interest to simply write off the wound or offense. This doesn't mean you pretend it didn't happen or that you don't think the offender should be held accountable. It simply means you refuse to spend any more of your time and energy on the matter. You decide to release it, let it go, leave it behind you—and move forward into your future.

1 Writing off a debt, whether it's financial or emotional, benefits the one who writes it off and the one whose debt is forgiven. Have you ever done this for someone? Has someone ever done it for you? What was the situation and how did it make you feel?

_____

_____

_____

_____

_____

_____

_____

_____

_____

_____

_____

2 Think about some of the situations that still cause you pain or anger. Are you willing to consider writing them off so you can loose yourself from them and embrace
the good things that are ahead of you? Circle yes or no.

Yes   No

Remember: "We must let go of demanding that the wrong be righted, the loss be restored, or the offender by punished in the way we deem appropriate" *(Let It Go,* p. 110).

What's the Value?

One of the main reasons people end up wounded, offended, and disappointed is that their values don't match the values of the person who hurt them. That may sound overly simple, but it's true. At the core of almost every offense is a difference in values.

Sometimes one person values a date enough to keep it and buy a new outfit for it while the other doesn't even value it enough to call and cancel; they just don't show up. Sometimes one person holds human life dear and precious, while another person values having a gun and feeling powerful by shooting someone else.

There are times we set ourselves up for trouble in a relationship because we assume another person shares the same values we hold dear. That's not always the case, and when we begin to see the differences, we need to know how to manage the situation or something unfortunate may develop.

None of us can change another person's value system. All we can do is clearly define our own values, express them appropriately, and protect them as best we can. And when our values are violated, we can respond in healthy, constructive ways—and then move on.

1 In the blanks below, write five things you value. They may be qualities like honesty; they may be tangible things like your life; they may be relationships or opportunities. Just think the things that are *really* important to you and jot them down.

_____

_____

_____

_____

_____

2 Think about a person with whom you've had conflict. If you think about that situation from the perspective of values, what were differences in the two of you? What did you value that they didn't? What did they value that you didn't?

_____

_____

_____

_____

_____

_____

_____

_____

_____

_____

_____

_____

3 Think about a relatively new relationship in your life. Who is this person, and as you're getting to know him or her, what values are you noticing? Are these values consistent with yours or not?

_____

_____

_____

_____

_____

_____

Remember: "Surely we all have similar moral fiber and are guided by a similar GPS as to the determination of fair and unfair, right and wrong, good and evil. Isn't that right? No, it absolutely is not" *(Let It Go,* p. 111).

Good Therapy

A personal offense or wound isn't easy to get over. Different things affect different people in different ways, and what may be a mere bump in the road of life for you may be a full-speed, debilitating crash for someone else.

When helping people on the journey toward forgiveness, I like to encourage them to back up a bit and gain some perspective on their problems. Focusing only on one's own troubles simply exacerbates the pain and tends to isolate a person from others, so it's always important to realize that you aren't the only one suffering and that, in fact, someone else may be suffering much more.

1 Because different people choose to handle situations in different kinds of ways, let's examine the way you choose to respond. When you encounter a hurt or an offense, you (check all that apply):

_____ think about it, but don't say much to anyone else

_____ try not to think about it or talk about it

_____ pick up the phone and share all the details with your best friend

_____ get out your journal and write about how hurt you are

_____ think about how bad it is and how much it hurts

_____ think about the fact that it isn't nearly as bad as what someone you know is going through

2 Are you dealing with a difficult development in your life? List two people who are going through things that are worse.

_____

_____

_____

3 The world is full of offense; some situations are even tragic and heartbreaking. Who do you know who has endured a serious offense that you consider devastating and has handled it well? How does the way he or she deals with the situation encourage and inspire you to deal with your own troubles?

_____

_____

_____

_____

_____

_____

_____

_____

_____

_____

_____

_____

_____

_____

_____

_____

_____

Remember: "One of the best therapies for those who think their life is shattered is to climb out of the narcissistic cocoon that pain incubates in and see how many people all around you have so much worse to overcome and do so with grace and tenacity" *(Let It Go,* p. 113).

In the Absence of an Apology . . .

I'm no expert on the statistical analysis of forgiveness, but I have a hunch that a high percentage of people who are currently suffering and stagnating in unforgiveness are doing so simply because they've demanded an apology they haven't received.

These people who demand an apology are often living in a fantasy world, because they're fixated on getting something that most likely is *not* going to happen. Let me explain why I seem so sure of this.

Most of the time, people who will disregard and devalue you to the point of committing a serious wrong against you or hurting you deeply do not care enough about you to apologize. Most people are so selfish, so self-focused, so caught up in their own little worlds that they hardly think about how their actions affect others. A lot of times, they don't even think an apology is in order!

For you to move forward, you'll need to realize that the pain and unforgiveness that are so difficult for you *are not hurting your offender at all.* You're going to have to give up that demand for an apology; accept the fact that you aren't going to get it; and decide to put the matter behind you.

1 Think about a specific person you wish would apologize to you. Check all the following characteristics that apply to that person. The more you check, the less likely you are to receive an apology.

_____ egotism, narcissism, or believing they are better than others

_____ showing little or no respect for other people's possessions

_____ borrowing money without repaying it

_____ borrowing anything without asking

_____ always trying to be first or not waiting their turn

_____ forgetting occasions that are important to you

_____ ignoring events that are important to you

_____ ignoring or minimizing your accomplishments

_____ speaking negatively to you or about you

_____ committing verbal, emotional, physical, or sexual abuse

_____ failing to carry out their responsibilities to you

_____ not keeping their word to you

2 Who do you believe owes you an apology? Answer me honestly: Do you think you're ever going to get it? Circle yes or no.

Yes   No

3 It's time now for a destiny-making decision. If you can let this situation go without an apology, you'll break the chains that bind you to it and hold you in the past. You'll set yourself free to run boldly into your future. What do you say: Will you make a decision right now to let go of the action that hurt or offended and of its the consequences, even if no one ever says "Sorry"? Circle yes or no.

Yes   No

4 Let's go one step further. Use the space below to put in writing—and date it—the fact that you choose today to forgive (person's name) for (specific offense). Then add something like, "I set myself free to explore and embrace the great future ahead of me!"

_____

_____

_____

_____

_____

_____

_____

_____

_____

_____

Remember: "The truth of the matter is there are some things that happen in life that you must forgive without the benefit of an apology, for your own emotional survival" (_Let It Go,_ p. 116).

Take Back Your Power

I've just asked you to do something you may have found difficult, but it's one of the most empowering actions you could ever take. You see, while you're waiting for someone to apologize, you are actually giving that person a lot of power. Every time you think about that person, he or she dominates your life.

When that happens, you deplete your energy and rob your mind of the chance to think good thoughts because you're locked into painful, angry thoughts. You forbid yourself to think about the positive relationships that can be yours in the future because you're focused on bad ones from the past. Taking back your power begins in your mind; it starts with your thoughts.

Once you begin to get your power back, I predict that you'll enjoy it so much you won't want to stop. In fact, I believe you'll just keep going and becoming more and more empowered until the journey of heartache you've been on becomes the fast track to your destiny!

1 What three thoughts are you going to have change if you are going to take back your power? As an example, you might have to stop thinking, "I cannot *believe* he did that to me!" Or you might have to refuse to think, "Because she did that to me, I will never be able to (fill in the blank)."

_____

_____

_____

_____

_____

_____

2 Look at the three thoughts you wrote in answer to question 1. The next thing to do is replace your negative thoughts with positive ones. For each of the thoughts you need to stop thinking, write down a constructive, power-filled thought with which you can replace it.

_____

_____

_____

_____

_____

_____

_____

_____

_____

_____

_____

_____

Remember: "What do you do when the persons who caused you the most pain have not and will not admit, acknowledge, or repent for their part in your pain? Simple answer, take the power back over your life and write it off" *(Let It Go,* p. 119).

Crucifixion Precedes Resurrection

The most powerful and pivotal story in the Christian faith is the account of Christ's crucifixion and resurrection (see Matthew 26–28). Crucifixion was a bloody, grueling, torturous form of death, but it was not the end of the journey for Christ or for those who place faith in him. The crucifixion was necessary in order to get to the resurrection. Christ knew this. He refused to focus on his pain and agony; he simply endured it and prayed that God would forgive those who persecuted him.

The crucifixion appeared to bring an end to a truly great and influential life. The killers had no idea that three days later, something awesome would happen—a glorious resurrection would take place and Christ would live again!

The pain you have suffered may not have resulted in your physical death, but perhaps it killed your dreams, murdered your self-esteem, stole your confidence, or stopped your emotional heart. I urge you today to believe that something awesome is ahead for you! A personal resurrection, a renewal of your life, a revival of your inner being, restoration of your vitality, and a new level of health and strength are on their way in your life!

1 What did the offense you suffered kill on the inside of you? How did it damage your heart/inner being?

_____

_____

_____

_____

_____

_____

2 Will you have the courage to believe that in spite of everything that has been damaged or destroyed, you can find new life? Circle yes or no.

Yes   No

Remember: "This is an extreme act of faith to believe that there is more ahead
of you than there is behind you. But at the end of the day, you will miss your
future swatting at your past" (*Let It Go*, p. 118).

Write It Off

If you look past the brutality of the offense you endured or the disappointment you suffered, what do you think your own personal type of resurrection and resurgence could be like? Take some time to dream about a bright
future and write down or represent in some other creative way the great hopes,
dreams, and goals you have for the months and years ahead.

Chapter 7
Help Wanted

Before you begin: Please familiarize yourself with Chapter 7 of Let It Go, *pages 121–135.*

The workplace. It's an environment where potential gets fulfilled, opportunities are realized, and accomplishments are often rewarded. For some people, the workplace is where their dreams come true. But all too often, the workplace is also an environment filled with competition, jealousy, and way too much stress. It's also often a place where unforgiveness runs rampant but not always recognized—and it can be detrimental to people's professional performance and even dangerous to their potential for promotion.

A lot of people these days feel that their work is stressful, and I sometimes wonder whether a good portion of the stress comes not from the tasks we must perform, but from the relationships surrounding them. We are around our coworkers, bosses, and employees *a lot*. So we need to know how to navigate the often choppy seas of the workplace with wisdom, strength, and grace.

1 Circle the words that describe the environment in your workplace.

Pleasant	Tense	Upbeat
Gloomy	Honest	Deceitful
Peaceful	Petty	Generous
Threatening	Trusting	Political
Happy	Contentious	Positive
Negative	Friendly	Hostile
Cliquish	Helpful	Difficult
Productive	Suspicious	Unwelcoming
Free	Mean-spirited	Supportive
Wounding	Fun	Manipulative
Respectful	Filled with conflict	Inspiring
With integrity	Gossipy	Caring
Cutthroat	Fair	With clear expectations
Healthy	Frustrating	Toxic

Now, count the number of positive words you circled and the number of negative words and put those numbers in the blanks below.

Positive: _____

Negative: _____

2 Based on the numbers above, is your workplace mostly positive or mostly negative?

_____

Remember: "With the exception of the marriage relationship, I would venture that no other environment produces more conflicts and requires more forgiveness than the place where we earn our living" *(Let It Go, pp. 121–122).*

Who's the Boss?

Almost everyone has a boss at some point in life. Whether you like it or not, the boss is the boss; this person is the one who makes sure you get paid. Whether or not you agree that this person should hold a position of leadership and authority is really irrelevant. The issue is how you relate to this person and making sure that no matter what challenges you face, you stay free from anger and resentment.

I want to ask you a few questions along these lines. As you answer them, think about either your current boss or a previous boss, but keep the same person in mind as you answer all the questions.

1 Have you ever been frustrated because you felt you were more competent or better equipped to lead than your boss is? Circle yes or no.

Yes   No

2 In your struggle with having to submit to your boss without necessarily agreeing with his or her leadership, have you been angry or become resentful? Circle yes or no.

Yes   No

3 Have you ever projected personal issues (such as a problem with authority or a need for leadership in your life) onto your relationship with your boss, even if you don't particularly like that person or feel they should hold their position? Circle yes or no.

Yes   No

4 If you have ever allowed your emotional baggage or issues to cause you to resent your boss or to make demands that he or she is not meant to fulfill, have you been angry or disappointed? Circle yes or no.

Yes   No

5 If you circled yes to question 2 or 4, realize that anger, resentment, and disappointment call for forgiveness. Are you willing to choose to forgive your boss? Circle yes or no.

Yes   No

Remember: "In an ideal world, those who lead and supervise us would be wiser, more experienced, and more mature than those under their supervision" (*Let It Go,* p. 125).

When You're the Boss—or You'd Like to Be

Being the person in charge is often the most challenging, frustrating job in the whole organization!

When a person steps into a position of authority and responsibility, all kinds of strange, unprecedented things take place. People who work for you may be biased against you without even giving you a chance. Or they may look to you to fill a leadership void in their lives or to meet a need that someone in their personal lives should fulfill. Many times, bosses get overworked because they not only have to do their jobs, they also have to deal with the whole host of the various issues and attitudes their subordinates bring to work. This can cause resentment and exasperation toward those who work for you.

1 Think about the employee who causes you the most trouble. What do you think this person's problem is? Is the problem directly work-related, or is it personal—and you just happen to be catching the fallout?

_____

_____

_____

_____

_____

_____

_____

_____

_____

2 On a typical workday, how do you handle this person?

_____ I try to avoid him or her.

_____ I make sure he or she is doing work to my satisfaction; then I leave that person alone.

_____ I grit my teeth and engage in a brief conversation once or twice a day.

_____ I understand the importance of building a positive relationship, so I'm trying to do that in an appropriate way and with good boundaries.

3 In question 2, the healthiest, most generous place we can get to is to try to build a positive relationship and to try to help the person grow. But you will never get there if you harbor pent-up frustration toward that person or resentment over having to deal with him or her. Are you willing to choose to forgive this person for their short-comings and seek a better relationship in the future? Circle yes or no.

Yes   No

Remember: "Leaders who find themselves embroiled in ongoing office tension often discover that the issue has nothing to do with them or their leadership style" (*Let It Go,* p. 124).

Practitioner or Manager?

Have you ever known someone who was an absolutely amazing salesman, who enjoyed his job, whose customers loved him, and whose company praised him for often exceeding his goals? Then the company promoted him to manager of the sales force, and before long, he was miserable and the people working for him didn't think they had a effective leader.

The kind of situation I've just described happens so often! And many times, the results are not good. This is relevant to forgiveness because an unhappy leader can be a bad leader, engendering resentment among their subordinates and making the leader unproductive and miserable. That person may need to forgive those who put them in the new position, and those who work for them may need to forgive them for not doing a good job—when they really aren't cut out to do a good job in that position.

You'll see two sets of questions below. The first set applies if you are responsible for leading or supervising others in your workplace. The second set applies if you work for someone else. If you are boss, but you also have a boss, you may want to answer both sets of questions. Here's a friendly, helpful hint: You might not want to work on this during your break and leave it open on your desk!

1 If you *are* a boss:

- Are you truly gifted to be a manager or an executive? Do your natural abilities lie in managing and leading others or are you better suited to be a practitioner? Check one.

_____ Manager

_____ Practitioner

- Answer honestly: Are you happier being a manager or executive than you were as a practitioner? Circle manager or practitioner.

  Manager   Practitioner

- On a scale of 1 to 10, how satisfied are you in your current position?

  1 = not at all; 10 = very much _____

- On a scale of 1 to 10, how much do you wish you could go back to practicing your true gifts and skills instead of managing or leading others?

  1 = not at all; 10 = very much _____

2 If you *have* a boss:

- Did your boss get promoted from a position of being a practitioner within your organization to being a manager or executive? Circle yes or no.

  Yes   No

- Answer honestly: Do you believe your boss is well suited for his or her job, or do you believe this person would excel more as a practitioner?

  Manager   Practitioner

- You may be a practitioner yourself. On a scale of 1 to 10, how well do you think you would perform the tasks involved in a managerial or executive role?

  1 = not well at all; 10 = exceptionally well _____

- On a scale of 1 to 10, how much would you enjoy being a manager or leader in your company?

  1 = not at all; 10 = very much _____

Remember this next time you're approached for a promotion. Don't let the promise of greater authority and a nice raise pull you away from doing what you're really good at and what you really enjoy!

Remember: "One of the regrettable practices within corporate America is that talented practitioners inevitably rise into management" *(Let It Go,* p. 125).

Go to the Source

When you have a grievance against someone, whether it's a minor complaint or a serious offense, go directly to that person first. Whether you need to resolve an issue with your boss or supervisor, someone on your team, someone who shares your cubicle, or someone who reports to you, the same approach is always best: Resist the urge to talk behind the person's back, and instead, go straight to the source of the problem. If the two of you need to get a mediator or higher-level leader involved to help at some point, then do, but try to work things out between yourselves first.

1 Do you have a problem you need to discuss with someone at work? What is the problem and who is the source? That's the person you need to start with.

_____

_____

_____

_____

_____

_____

_____

2 In *Let It Go* (p. 127), I suggest that you write a letter in which you honestly articulate the grudges you hold against your supervisor. This would also work if you have a problem with a coworker or a subordinate. Why not take some time to do that now on a separate sheet of paper?

Remember: "The temptation will be strong to talk behind his or her back, to complain, grumble, and even gossip because of the offense that festers within you. You must resist this common quagmire of corporate unforgiveness by first speaking with the person who offended you, not with everyone else" *(Let It Go,* p. 127).

Conflict and Confrontation

No matter what a situation entails, when conflict arises, you're going to have to deal with another human being in order to resolve it.

There are a few things to keep in mind when you need to confront someone. First, as you know by now, focus on the issue and not the person. While you may need to point out something someone has done wrong, do so in a way that highlights the action, not the individual. Second, never enter into a confrontation with preconceived notions or expectations about how the other person will respond. Let the confrontation unfold however it unfolds, dealing with each aspect of it as you go instead of playing out how you *think* it will go in your mind before it happens.

1 Is there a situation in your workplace right now that you know you need to confront, but you've been putting it off? What is it?

_____

_____

_____

_____

_____

_____

2 What specific steps will you take to confront the conflict you're currently dealing with?

_____

_____

_____

_____

———————————————————————

———————————————————————

———————————————————————

———————————————————————

———————————————————————

———————————————————————

———————————————————————

Remember: "You must never assume that you know how a confrontation will go in the workplace" *(Let It Go, p. 129).*

For Your Toolbox

The best way to get any job done is to use the right tool. For example, if you need to drive a nail into a board, you don't pick up a socket wrench; you grab a hammer. This same principle applies when you need to confront someone.

Experts say there are five basic ways to handle conflict, and I believe all five are essential tools; they're simply needed at different times in different situations, just like the hammer and the wrench. You can read about them in greater detail on pages 129–131 of *Let It Go,* but let me list them here. They are: avoiding, commanding, accommodating, compromising, and collaborating.

1 Write briefly about a situation in which you have used or could currently use the conflict resolution tool listed.

Avoiding:

_____

_____

_____

_____

_____

Commanding:

_____

_____

_____

_____

_____

Accommodating:

_____

_____

_____

_____

_____

_____

Compromising:

_____

_____

_____

_____

_____

_____

Collaborating:

_____

_____

_____

_____

_____

_____

2 In this workbook, I have mentioned your default settings. Do you have a default setting when it comes to when trying to resolve conflict? Which one is it? Check one:

_____ avoiding

_____ commanding

_____ accommodating

_____ compromising

_____ collaborating

3 Why is it important to move beyond your default setting and use different methods of conflict resolution under different circumstances?

_____

_____

_____

_____

_____

_____

Remember: "All five of these styles of handling conflict are effective in the right situation" *(Let It Go,* p. 131).

Creating a Positive, Productive Work Environment

The workplace is not a neat little neighborhood defined by manicured hedges so everyone can stay in their place; it's a dynamic, fluid conglomeration of people who bring a variety of talents, skills, visions, strategies—and personal issues.

It's the personal issues that most often create the need for forgiveness. No one is immune to them. Your coworkers have theirs and you have yours. At some point, as all of you come together to create, produce, promote, or sell some great product or service, those issues will raise their ugly heads. Many times, the core of the issue will be some type of offense and the antidote for it will be forgiveness.

I want be sure you understand the three things forgiveness empowers you to experience and do on the job. First, being able to extend and receive forgiveness will enable you to enjoy and be fulfilled in your job. Second, forgiveness will improve your chances for promotion and advancement. Third, if you want to be a leader in your company or any organization, being able to forgive others and receive forgiveness from them is essential.

1 How can being able to give and receive forgiveness bring greater job fulfillment to you personally?

_____

_____

_____

_____

2 How can being able to give and receive forgiveness improve the possibility that you will be promoted on your job?

_____

_____

_____

_____

3 How can being able to give and receive forgiveness help position and prepare you to become a leader in your company or industry?

_____

_____

_____

_____

_____

Remember: "Practicing forgiveness allows you to be fulfilled by your job . . . increases your opportunities for promotion and advancement . . . [and] equips you to be a leader when opportunities present themselves" (*Let It Go,* p. 135).

Write It Off

In an ideal world, your job should be a place where you can use your gifts and talents, fulfill your potential, and work in a supportive environment that encourages your professional growth and development. Think about the things that are really important to you in a job and then express your thoughts and feelings about two things: 1) how you will prioritize and grow in the things that matter to you, even though your current job may place some limitations on that; and 2) what you will look for when you're in the market for a new job.

Chapter 8
Trust Doesn't Come Easy

Before you begin: Please familiarize yourself with Chapter 8 of Let It Go, *pages 137–149.*

Once we've endured an offense and chosen to forgive, we have another decision to make: Will we stay as involved in the relationship as we were before the offense, and if so, how can we trust the offender again? I want to take a moment now to emphasize that forgiving someone does not mean you should forget about the offense and resume the relationship as it used to be. And most importantly, it does not mean you have to, or should, trust the person who hurt you. No, your trust is a precious commodity and you must give it cautiously and wisely. When people break your trust, they need to earn it back.

You see, you only have one set of circumstances to help you decide whether to trust again not: the person's past actions—not their words, not their good intentions—*their actions*. To regain your trust the offender must demonstrate consistent, changed behaviors that create positive experiences for you. These cannot be temporary changes intended to win you back; they must be experi-

ences that come from a truly repentant heart and are positive enough and
regular enough to inspire you to take a risk with this person again.

1 Describe a situation in which you feel you have forgiven someone, but now you
  need to know how to move forward and rebuild trust.

_____

_____

_____

_____

_____

_____

_____

_____

_____

_____

_____

2 In your own words, describe the difference between forgiving someone and trusting someone.

_____

_____

_____

_____

_____

_____

_____

_____

_____

_____

_____

Remember: "Understand that trust is a valuable commodity that cannot be purchased with credit" *(Let It Go,* p. 137).

Whose Job Is It?

There are certain choices you must make if you want to move into your future with freedom and joy, such as the choice to forgive and the choice to cautiously wade back into a relationship with someone. But the responsibility for rebuilding trust belongs to the person who did damage to your soul. You certainly have to be willing to trust again, but it's the offender's job to earn it.

You see, you trusted that person at one time—and you got burned! You're smart to move slowly and deliberately, and you're smart to pay close attention to the person's words and actions to make sure they align and to make sure they reveal an honest intention to regain your trust.

1 Think about someone who hurt or offended you and now wants to restore the relationship. What is he or she doing right now to make a sincere effort to rebuild trust?

_____

_____

_____

_____

_____

2 Think about the person who came to mind when you answered question 1 and consider what this person says and does. For example, do they say, "I want to work on this relationship," and then go off with their friends or talk badly about you behind your back? In the space below, write down a few things the person who hurt you says to you, then write down whether he or she actually makes good on those things.

_____

_____

_____

_____

_____

_____

_____

_____

_____

_____

_____

Remember: "Trust when damaged can be rebuilt, but the trust builder has to be willing to punch the clock and do the time to rebuild what was lost in the fall" *(Let It Go,* p. 139).

It Takes Time

In an instant, often in just a few seconds, a person can say or do something that destroys a relationship that took years to build. When that person calms down and cools off, they may feel much better after releasing so much anger that they are ready to patch things up quickly and move on. The problem is, when you have been deeply hurt, even if the wound was inflicted in just a few seconds, you're not likely to be eager to patch things up. You may feel that so much damage has been done that a major rebuilding process is necessary and you may recognize that it's going to take time.

1 Are you in a situation right now in which someone wants to rebuild a relationship and go on much faster than you do? Circle yes or no.

Yes   No

2 Do you understand that as the one who was hurt, you have a right to move at a pace that's comfortable for you? Do you realize you do not have to be rushed? Circle yes or no.

Yes   No

3 In the space below, jot down some of the things you need and want in a relationship that may be in the process of being restored and record your honest, current impressions of whether the person will be able to deliver or not.

_____

_____

_____

_____

_____

_____

_____

_____

_____

_____

_____

4 If you are the one who injured someone else emotionally, I'd like to give you a chance now to answer some questions I asked in *Let It Go.* As you think about how long it may take to rebuild trust, consider the following:

- How deep was the wound?

  _____

  _____

  _____

  _____

  _____

- How quickly does the victim normally heal?

  _____

  _____

  _____

  _____

  _____

- How patient are you to allow him or her to cry, vent, complain, and go through mood swings and everything else to regain their trust?

_____

_____

_____

_____

_____

Remember: "Most people who have violated a trust have a tendency to minimize how long it takes to rebuild it. . . . The person who has violated the trust must be prepared to walk down the long road to healing" *(Let It Go,* p. 140).

It's *Not* All in the Family

You know by now that forgiveness does not equal forgetting an offense and that it does not mean you have to restore your trust in the person who hurt or offended you. I want to take this one step farther and say that not trusting someone doesn't mean you don't love them. You can absolutely love someone without trusting them!

I like to say you can love someone without trusting them and you can also love them without giving them everything they ask for. Keep this in mind as you deal with your friends and family members, especially when trust has been violated once and they ask you to trust them again because, after all, "we're family!"

1 Even in families, where people are "supposed" to support and even sacrifice for one another, good boundaries are still needed. Is there someone in your family who wants things from you that you aren't willing to give? Who is it and how can you say no in a nice, but firm, way?

_____

_____

_____

_____

_____

2 Have you ever noticed that Scripture never commands us to trust people; it only commands us to love them and forgive them? In a specific relationship, in practical ways, what does this mean to you?

_____

_____

_____

_____

_____

_____

_____

_____

_____

_____

_____

_____

Remember: "Real love has nothing to do with trust. Neither does forgiveness. It is highly possible to love someone you do not trust" *(Let It Go,* p. 142).

Construction Crew

If you've ever seen a building rebuilt after some devastating natural disaster, you know that it takes a lot of people to get it done. The same idea applies when trust needs to be rebuilt in a relationship. Trust can't do all the work by itself; it needs some help and the best helpers are honesty, understanding, consistency, and communication. I explain these on page 143 of *Let it Go,* if you'd like to read more about them.

1 As you think about a relationship in which trust needs to be rebuilt, in what ways
   do you think honesty will help? What do you and the one who hurt you need to
discuss frankly, openly, and honestly?

_____

_____

_____

_____

_____

_____

_____

_____

_____

_____

_____

2 What do you need to understand about the person who offended you and what does that person need to understand about you in order to rebuild trust?

_____

_____

_____

_____

_____

_____

_____

_____

_____

_____

_____

3 Consistency is important in the process of rebuilding trust. How are you going to monitor the offender's behavior to see whether he or she is being consistent?

_____

_____

_____

_____

_____

_____

Positioning Yourself for the Future

When you are reeling from a deep wound or disappointment, or from a past wound that gets reinjured, you go through all kinds of thoughts and emotions. One of them is a question like this: "How could I trust someone who's now so obviously *not* trustworthy?" You may wonder how you missed some kind of evidence that the person would betray you, and get caught in a self-destructive cycle of trying to justify your choice to be in a relationship with that person while also telling yourself the lie that you are stupid.

This kind of thought pattern can be hard to break, but it's *vital* that you do so. In order to move forward into the bright and promising future that stretches out before you, you must regain your trust in yourself. To move forward with strength, you have to have confidence in yourself and in your judgments about people. Know that you won't be able to assess them with 100 percent accuracy every time, but also realize that everything you've been through has taught you valuable lessons about life and relationships—and that you are constantly growing in the emotional and mental resources you need to make great decisions about relationships in the future.

1 Typically, when someone wounds or offends you, how do you respond? Check all that apply.

_____ I beat up on myself and wonder why I ever trusted that person in the first place.

_____ I wonder what I did to cause that person to hurt me.

_____ I ask the rhetorical question: "What on earth is *wrong* with that person?"

_____ I decide something *is* wrong with that person and I move on.

2 If you checked the first or second option in question 1, you're in good company. A lot of people respond by doubting themselves and chastising themselves for making a bad relational decision. Are you willing to forgive yourself for that and believe that you and this person simply ended up in a bad situation or misunderstanding, which doesn't mean you did anything wrong at all? Circle yes or no.

Yes   No

3 Now's a good time to make a decision that will serve you well in the future. Commit today to believe in yourself in a healthy way, to refuse to allow other people's negative actions to make you doubt your judgment, and to believe great opportunities

and great relationships are in store for you! Write down your commitment in the space provided.

_____

_____

_____

_____

_____

_____

_____

_____

_____

_____

_____

_____

Remember: "More times than not, the victim [loses] confidence in their own ability to discern what is true. This is often the most difficult aspect of the process" *(Let It Go, p. 144)*.

What's Left?

When you want to rebuild a damaged relationship, you have to start by looking at what you and the other person still have, not at what you lost. For example, in a marriage, two people may have lost some trust in each other, but they realize they still have love. In a work relationship, people may not even like each other after an offense, but they realize they both respect the other's professional skills and abilities. In cases where there is something valuable left, focus on that and rebuild from there.

1 Are you in a situation in which you've lost a lot, but something is still there? What's left?

_____

_____

_____

_____

_____

_____

2 Is what's left valuable enough to you and strong enough in the relationship to serve as a new foundation on which you can rebuild? Circle yes or no.

Yes   No

Remember: *"No one rebuilds on what they lost.* Rebuilding begins when you appreciate what you have left" *(Let It Go,* p. 145).

Difficult, but Worth It

The world is full of stories of anger and revenge. Some of them are appalling. But the world is also full of stories of love and forgiveness—and some of those are breathtaking. I want to tell you today that you can have a breathtaking story if you want to.

I am not saying you need to forgive someone who remains dangerous to you just so you can talk about the drama of doing so. I am encouraging you to be wise and cautious as you restore relationships and rebuild trust, but also to keep a few things in mind. First, be aware that your offender may be much more remorseful than you know. They may not be good at showing it, but they may be suffering immensely over the pain they caused you.

Second, remember that a person may do something out of personal weakness, but that doesn't mean he or she is "bad" or intended to damage your soul.

Third, realize that being open to rebuild trust and restore a relationship takes courage and character. It takes a person of great heart to do that.

Fourth, understand that you may find treasures in another person and in a relationship as you go through the process of rebuilding.

I'll close this chapter with these thoughts, knowing you may need some time to process them. I know that restoring a relationship after a terrible offense or deep wound takes lots of courage, time, and energy. I know it can be emotionally grueling at times. But I also know that it can be worth every bit of effort it requires.

1 Is there a chance that the person who hurt you may be feeling more pain over the incident than you realize? Are you willing to believe that's possible? Circle yes or no.

Yes   No

2 What does this thought mean to you: "There is a difference between weakness and wickedness"?

_____

_____

_____

_____

_____

_____

3 Why do you think it takes a person of character and courage to be willing to rebuild trust in a broken relationship? Are you willing to try?

_____

_____

_____

_____

_____

_____

_____

Remember: "There is a difference between weakness and wickedness" (*Let It Go,* p. 148)

Write It Off

When the time comes to restore trust after a relationship has been broken, some people are more eager to do so than others. Write, draw, or otherwise express how you really feel about going back into the relationship. Don't even consider what other people think you should do; express what's in your heart. If it's extreme reluctance, that's okay!

Chapter 9
Recovery Rate

Before you begin: Please familiarize yourself with Chapter 9 of Let It Go, *pages 151–167.*

There are two sides to every story. I'm sure you've heard that before. But when you're the one who's been deeply wounded, even though the one who hurt you has a story, seeing the other person's perspective can be almost impossible. Your hurt and anger may not only cause you not to care about the other person's point of view; they may cause you to also look at his or her side of things through a cloudy filter of pain that keeps you from seeing the truth.

The truth as it really is, is this: Most people don't intentionally set out to offend or devastate others. Most of the time it just happens—sometimes in an unexpected moment of anger or pain, and at other times completely inadvertently—and the person doesn't even know you're hurt until you mention it.

You may have heard the saying, "Hurting people hurt people." It's true: When people haven't healed from their own emotional wounds or resolved their own personal issues, they tend to inflict pain upon the hearts of others.

1 Have you ever been really hurt by someone and then come to realize that person
hurt you not because of malicious intent, but because he or she was so deeply
wounded? Circle yes or no.

Yes   No

2 If you answered yes to question 1, describe the situation you were thinking of.
How did you come to recognize the offender's pain and woundedness?

_____

_____

_____

_____

_____

_____

_____

_____

_____

_____

3 Were you able to forgive the offender you were thinking of in questions 1 and 2 once you understood that he or she hurt you more because of their pain than because of anything you did wrong? Circle yes or no. If not, you could choose to forgive right now!

Yes   No

Remember: "Most of us end up hurt by someone who wasn't even intending to hurt us, but their selfishness, egotism, and entitlement left us injured in the wake of their collateral damage" *(Let It Go,* p. 152).

Roll Call for the Wounded Warriors

People who hurt others out of their own pain typically fall into one of three categories: the insulators, the isolators, and the inhibitors. All of these people turn their wounded rage inward so it may not be readily visible to others, but it's still damaging. Since you can read about them in detail on pages 156–159 of *Let It Go*—and I encourage you to do so now—I will simply mention them here. They are insulators, isolators, and inhibitors.

1 Think about yourself. Which type of wounded warrior do you tend to be? Check one:

_____ an insulator

_____ an isolator

_____ an inhibitor

2 Think about someone who has hurt you deeply. What type of wounded warrior is this person?

_____ an insulator

_____ an isolator

_____ an inhibitor

3 Given the type of wounded warrior you are, what steps might you take to become stronger and more whole, so you reduce the possibility of hurting other people unintentionally?

_____

_____

_____

_____

_____

_____

Remember: "If you have ever been the victim of someone whose weaknesses have left you feeling murdered in heart, soul, or body, part of the healing begins when you understand that most perpetrators are themselves victims" (*Let It Go,* p. 156).

Big Bullies

When we talk about people who hurt other people, we cannot ignore a group that has gained much attention recently because of their harmful behavior: bullies. In recent years, the tremendous problem of bullying has been in the spotlight because it has become so severe in some places that people—children and teenagers—have killed themselves over it. It must stop!

Unlike the other wounded warriors I have mentioned (insulators, isolators, and inhibitors), bullies turn their wounded rage outward, against others, instead of inward toward themselves. Simply put, my definition of a bully is someone who belittles or intimidates others to make himself or herself seem big or powerful. This can happen emotionally, physically, or verbally. And it's not limited to elementary schoolrooms or high-school locker rooms. It also happens in corporate boardrooms and in the bedrooms of married couples. It seems to be as prevalent among adults as it is among young people—and it is wrong in every situation.

1 Have you ever encountered a bully? Circle yes or no.

Yes   No

2 If you answered yes to question 1, how did you feel when you were bullied?

_____

_____

_____

_____

_____

_____

_____

3 Have you ever displayed any qualities of a bully, specifically trying to make your-self seem big by intimidating someone else or trying to make them feel small? If so, what were the circumstances, and how are you going to keep from doing that in the future?

_____

_____

_____

_____

_____

_____

_____

_____

_____

_____

_____

Remember: "Let us be clear that bullying doesn't just occur on playgrounds or in school systems, or as isolated behavior in hormonal adolescents" *(Let It Go,* p. 160).

You Can Recover and Move Ahead!

Just about everyone who is wounded or offended becomes, on some level, an insulator, an isolator, an inhibitor, or a bully. Now, before you get offended by my saying that, understand that it's just true. Everyone responds to pain in some way (otherwise, we wouldn't be human), and typically, it's one of those four. The good news is: We can break free from the way we currently handle our pain and begin to manage it in healthier ways. We can recover and experience less lingering pain and more lasting joy in the future!

The key to moving beyond where you are right now into a stronger, healthier place is being willing to deal with your own shortcomings and weaknesses and being willing to move ahead and take risks again in the future. The quicker you remove anger, offense, and bitterness from your heart, the faster you can move forward.

1 Here is where the rubber meets the road. Are you willing to acknowledge and wrestle with the unhealthy ways you have dealt with pain in the past? Circle yes or no.

Yes   No

2 Based on what you've learned in *Let It Go* and in this workbook, or in other settings, what are the most negative and unhealthy ways you have handled painful
situations in the past?

_____

_____

_____

_____

_____

_____

3 Emotionally and relationally, what would "a state of healthy functionality" look
like in your life?

_____

_____

_____

_____

_____

_____

_____

_____

_____

_____

_____

Remember: "Instead of driving us inward to insulate, isolate, or inhibit, our anger over having a weakened heart from an unexpected injury can become the fuel for our recovery" (*Let it Go,* p. 164).

Understanding Is Powerful

I believe the next important step in your recovery, after admitting the negative ways you've dealt with emotional pain in the past and being willing to change and grow to deal with them better in the future, is to really make an effort to understand the person who hurt you.

To get to the truth of the matter, you'll probably have to have an honest conversation with the offender. The only way you can really know what that person was thinking or what motivated them is to let them tell you. When they do, do two things: 1) Do your best to put yourself in their position, because that can go a long way toward helping you understand why they spoke or acted as they did; and 2) focus on feelings, not behavior. You'll have to focus on behavior at some point, but in the process of gaining understanding, if you'll try to see how the person *felt,* you may better understand what they did.

1 Will you schedule a conversation with the person who hurt or offended you? If so, how will you try to gain understanding about what he or she did to hurt you?

_____

_____

_____

_____

_____

_____

_____

_____

_____

2 Let's do an exercise. Take a situation—something that has actually happened to you or something you've observed in someone else's life. Write down what happened, then list what you think could have been the offender's best possible intentions (even though they may have gone wrong). This is good training for learning to believe the best about people and understand them—and that will help you immensely in relationships.

_____

_____

_____

_____

_____

_____

_____

_____

_____

_____

_____

Remember: "Through understanding, returning to the scene of the offense and standing under the person who has hurt us, we free ourselves by gaining insight into our perpetrator's intentions" *(Let It Go,* pp. 164–165).

Let Them Go

Before we close this chapter, I want to take a moment to acknowledge that many people have unforgiveness issues with their parents. This may be true for you. Some harbor anger because their fathers were absent or away much of the time; some are resentful because their mothers were too demanding; some feel both of their parents favored a sibling over them. The list of parental offenses is long and the wounds are deep.

Let me simply say that chances are your parents did the best they could, given the pressures they were under, the limitations they faced, and/or the wounds they carried in their own hearts. One of the greatest gifts you can give yourself, and your parents, is the gift of forgiveness. Choose today to release the anger, disappointment, or resentment you've held for years. Simply let it go. Set your parents free and set yourself free!

1   Now that you are older and perhaps a parent yourself, what do you understand about your parents that you didn't understand as a child or a teenager?

_____

_____

_____

_____

_____

_____

_____

_____

_____

2 Use the space below to write several sentences that begin with these eight words: "I choose today to forgive my parents for," then finish the sentence with specific things that hurt or offended you. If you need to, use as much space as is provided here and continue on a separate sheet of paper.

_____

_____

_____

_____

_____

_____

_____

_____

_____

_____

_____

_____

_____

Remember: "Rare is the parent who does not at least attempt to do their best for their child, even if their best effort is limited beyond their control" *(Let It Go,* p. 165).

Write It Off

Even when you know in your mind that a person never meant to harm you or maybe even had good intentions that ended up hurting you, that doesn't necessarily take away the pain in your heart. Think about a specific offense or disappointment in which you ended up as the victim of a well-meaning person. Using words, pictures, photographs, or any other creative medium you'd like, describe the pain. Getting it out is the first step toward becoming whole!

Chapter 10
Mercy Me

Before you begin: Please familiarize yourself with Chapter 10 of Let It Go, *pages 169–182.*

When one person extends mercy or compassion to another, especially when to someone who could have understandably deserved to "get in trouble," it's a relief. But when God—the Supreme, All-Powerful Being of the universe—extends divine mercy when judgment would have been appropriate, it's *awesome.*

You see, God's character is amazing. He has an absolutely perfect balance of mercy and justice. He is righteous; he is capable of anger; and he can be offended. But at the same time, woven into every fiber of his very nature is a flow of mercy, compassion, love, and forgiveness; he would rather dispense these things than execute wrath. In fact, we could say mercy is God's default setting. It is always his first choice in dealing with us; and it's his second, third, and fourth choice, on into infinity!

1 Which of the phrases below describe your concept of God? Check all that apply.

_____ a strict disciplinarian

_____ a distant overseer

_____ a harsh judge eager to punish

_____ a wise ruler eager to be kind

_____ one who doesn't pay attention to me

_____ one who knows and cares about my every thought and action

_____ one who wants to scold me for my mistakes

_____ one who wants me to learn and grow from my mistakes

_____ one who leaves me to figure out life on my own

_____ one who intentionally leads me into good things as life unfolds

2 If your concept of God has never acknowledged the great mercy inherent in his character, are you willing to change your thinking and believe that he is merciful and that he wants to be merciful to you in every possible way? Circle yes or no.

Yes   No

3 Have you ever had a personal experience with God's mercy? Describe it.

_____

_____

_____

_____

_____

_____

_____

_____

_____

_____

_____

Remember: "Our God isn't just powerful and righteous, but he is also merciful and compassionate. It is not just that he acts mercifully toward us, his children, but mercy is at the very heart of who he is" (*Let It Go*, p. 170).

New Every Morning

There's an incredibly powerful declaration of truth in the Old Testament Book of Lamentations. Take a look at this: "It is of the LORD's mercies that we are not consumed, because his compassions fail not. They are new every morning" (3:22–23). This is great news! Though God will not allow willful, ongoing, intentional disregard for his authority, he has obligated himself in his Word to completely forget yesterday's wrongdoings and happily dispense a fresh dose of mercy to us every single day. And because there are no perfect people on earth (only those who *think* they are), we all live in need of such a gracious provision.

We need to understand something about mercy if we're going to receive it and experience it every day. We need to know that God's mercy is not simply being nice. It's far deeper, richer, and more divine than that. It is absolute, unconditional forgiveness, complete with totally forgetting your offense, extended to you by the one Being in the universe who could dispense anger and punishment if he wanted to. But he doesn't. He wants you to see what you did wrong, be sorry, and repent (ask his forgiveness) for it and learn and grow from your mistake. He'd much rather bless you in spite of your offenses than punish you for them.

1 Think about the last several days. Have you been absolutely *perfect,* or have you done some things that make you glad God is merciful? In what ways have you needed mercy recently?

_____

_____

_____

_____

_____

_____

_____

_____

_____

_____

_____

2 In your own words, what does this phrase from *Let It Go* mean to you: "[God's] mercy is the defense attorney that releases us from the prosecuting attorney of his justice" (p. 171)?

_____

_____

_____

_____

_____

3 How do you think God's mercy differs from human kindness?

_____

_____

_____

_____

_____

_____

_____

_____

_____

_____

Remember: "God doesn't withhold his love until we are mature and developed. Instead he lavishly commends his love while we are yet sinners to show us the one real taste of unconditional love from the one source entitled to judge us that doesn't" *(Let It Go, p. 172)*.

Trickle Down

The Bible is full of great stories. One of them is in Matthew's Gospel, and it tells of a servant whose master forgave him an enormous debt. You can read about it on pages 173–174 of *Let It Go*. The point of the story is to show us how lavish God is in his forgiveness toward us—and how we, in turn, can be very stingy when it comes to forgiving others. Jesus tells the story to inspire us to remember how merciful God is to us and to honor that mercy by extending it to others.

Also in Matthew's Gospel is the Lord's Prayer. You may know it by memory, but do you know it contains a dangerous line? Let me explain. In the prayer, we say, "Forgive us our trespasses as we forgive those who trespass against us." The idea here is similar to Jesus's story about the servant, except that in the prayer we are asking God to treat us the same way we treat others. This is serious stuff!

So you can see from Jesus's story about the servant and from the Lord's Prayer that when we receive the forgiveness God so freely gives us, we need to be sure to extend that same forgiveness, freely and fully, to others.

1 Have you ever felt that you forgave someone in a pretty major way and then that person refused to forgive you for something fairly minor? Circle yes or no.

Yes   No

2 If you answered yes to question 1, how did you feel when that person wasn't merciful toward you when you had been so merciful toward him or her?

_____

_____

_____

_____

_____

_____

_____

_____

_____

3 Have you been as merciful to others as God has been to you? Circle your honest
answer, yes or no.

Yes   No

4 Most people realize they have not been as merciful to others as God has been to
them. If that's you, how can you become more merciful? You could answer this
in general terms or with specific steps you can take right now in a situation with a
certain person.

_____

_____

_____

_____

_____

_____

_____

_____

_____

_____

_____

Remember: "When you and I consider how much God (who knows everything there is to know about us) still forgives us, covers us, and keeps us, how can we then find within ourselves the audacity to condemn others?" *(Let It Go,* pp. 173–174).

Power Trip

You are in a serious power seat when you have an opportunity to forgive and extend mercy to someone. You have a clear choice to make, and that choice will impact another person's life and your own life in profound ways, perhaps long into the future. At times, knowing you have that much influence can give you a major attitude. But before you get a big head, you need to know something: God is watching.

You see, few tests in life reveal a person's character as clearly as the power test. What I mean by that is that people show their true colors when they have a chance to wield power over others, especially in personal relationships.

God is enormously interested in your character because he knows your character is directly related to the way you will handle his blessings. When he puts a spotlight on your character, it's not because he's looking for something in you to punish; he's looking to bless you. When he sees that you can be trusted to dispense mercy and forgiveness—well, let me just say, that's a plus!

I encourage you to train your brain to default to mercy. Next time you're in a position of power because someone has hurt or offended you and asked your forgiveness, don't think immediately about the offense and how it wounded you. Instead, think first about how much mercy God has poured out to you—and you'll be more likely to rush to pour out mercy on the person who needs it from you.

1 In your own words, describe why being in a position to be merciful and forgiving to someone—or not—is a place of power.

_____

_____

_____

_____

_____

_____

_____

_____

_____

_____

_____

2 How can you train your brain to default to mercy more quickly and more completely?

_____

_____

_____

_____

_____

_____

Remember: "As Jesus said in the Beatitudes, 'Blessed are the merciful for they shall obtain mercy'" *(Let It Go,* p. 178).

Rock Your World

Simply put, in the story of Scripture's most stunning and powerful example of forgiveness, a woman gets caught in adultery. You can refresh your memory about it on pages 178–179 of *Let It Go*.

In the story, Jesus was not nearly as concerned about the woman's sin as he was about the importance of her learning not to sin again. He wasn't trying to get her to stop acting bad, he was trying to inspire her to live a life free from the torment of secret sex and the shame it brought her. He just wanted her to learn a lesson.

When you and I commit offenses, Jesus wants the same for us. He doesn't want to berate us; he simply wants us to learn not to do those things again, so he can do great things for us.

1 What does the story of the woman who was caught in adultery teach you about Jesus's character? Scripture says he never changes (see Hebrews 13:8). His forgiving and merciful heart toward her is the same as his heart toward you.

_____

_____

_____

_____

_____

_____

_____

_____

2 Think about a situation in which someone forgave you or let you off the hook for
something that was really hurtful or that really caused a problem. What did you
learn from that about the importance of being merciful to others?

_____

_____

_____

_____

_____

_____

_____

_____

Remember: "We should learn from our mistakes, not crawl back into bed with them" *(Let It Go,* p. 179).

Infinite Chances

When we hear about someone who's been given a second chance, we tend to think it's great. And it is. But what's even greater is to be given an infinite number of chances, and that's what God does when he forgives.

While God certainly doesn't want us to go around deliberately doing wrong, he does look at our hearts (our motives and intentions), and when he sees that we make honest mistakes and are genuinely sorry, he is glad to forgive us and help us learn from them, so we can know better, do better, and be blessed in the future.

1 Have you ever been given a second chance? What did that feel like?

_____

_____

_____

_____

_____

_____

_____

_____

2 Is there someone in your life who needs a second chance—or a third, fourth, or two thousandth chance? Who is that person and why is it important for you to give him or her another chance in a wise way that will not damage yourself or someone else?

_____

_____

_____

_____

_____

_____

_____

Remember: "If you have been forgiven there is no need to walk in guilt. Choose rather to walk in the wisdom that avoids foolish repetition of the same mistake made over and over again" *(Let It Go,* p. 182).

Write It Off

With words, pictures, or whatever creative means you desire, express what true mercy means to you.

Chapter 11
Love Thy Neighbor as Thyself

Before you begin: Please familiarize yourself with Chapter 11 of Let It Go, *pages 183–197.*

You may remember the story in *Let It Go* of my friend who became his own stumbling block on the road to success. That occurs more often than we might think. The best that can happen in the midst of it is that we recognize our tendencies to self-sabotage. Then we can do something about them and avoid them in the future.

One way we help ourselves instead of hurting ourselves is to learn to forgive ourselves and to love ourselves in a healthy way. An appropriate self-love, including the ability to forgive yourself for both your little mistakes and your big failures, will take you a long way toward success in every area of your life.

1 Have you ever jeopardized or stood in the way of your own success? What happened?

_____

_____

_____

_____

_____

_____

2 Can you think of a few ways you can avoid self-sabotage in the future?

_____

_____

_____

_____

_____

_____

_____

_____

_____

_____

Remember: "I believe we often stand in the way of our own success, both personally and professionally" *(Let It Go,* p. 185).

Be Your Own Best Friend

The way you feel about yourself is enormously important. Whether you realize it or not, it can affect your potential to get a job and your ability to get promoted once you have a job. Your self-image also has a tremendous effect on whether you are able to participate in a healthy marriage, whether you can be a good friend, and whether you can be a fair and loving parent.

I urge you to focus on your good qualities and learn to love yourself, accept yourself, and extend to yourself the same mercy God extends to you. You are valuable to God, to the people who love you, and to the world. You are worth taking care of, and you are a person who deserves to enjoy life, live it to the fullest, and succeed in every way.

I want to issue you a challenge today: Become your own best friend, and become your own cheerleader. Treat yourself well; acknowledge your worth; be kind to yourself; and believe you can reach the great destiny for which you were created.

1 Can you honestly say that you love yourself? Circle yes or no.

Yes   No

2 Which of the positive traits listed below are true about you? Circle all that apply.

Accepting	Authentic	Capable
Caring	Courageous	Compassionate
Creative	Dependable	Eager to learn
Efficient	Energetic	Friendly
Fun to be around	Funny	Gentle
Good in a crisis	Helpful	Honest
Industrious	Interesting	Kind
Lighthearted	Loyal	Open-minded
Organized	Patient	Positive
Proactive	Productive	Resourceful
Respectful	Responsible	Smart
Strong	Thoughtful	Trustworthy
Understanding	Upbeat	With integrity

3 Do you have other good qualities not listed above? If so, list them here. Then list your five best qualities and write a little bit about how each one is revealed in your life or personality.

_____

_____

_____

_____

_____

_____

_____

_____

_____

_____

Remember: "Many of us find ourselves consumed by self-contempt and diverted from allowing our gifts to be used as God intended by our unwillingness to forgive ourselves" *(Let It Go,* p. 185).

The Most Important Person to Forgive

When we think about the sometimes heinous things people can do to each other, it's a bit odd that we find forgiving another person's gross and grievous offenses can be easier than forgiving our own. And yet, many people say they struggle to forgive themselves much more than they do to forgive others.

Perhaps this is because we see so painfully, firsthand, what some of our mistakes or misjudgments have cost us; we know the price we've paid. Perhaps we live with daily physical or emotional reminders of the consequences of our bad decisions in our own lives or the lives of those we love. Perhaps we simply cannot shake the guilt we feel. Or perhaps it's because many of us are just naturally wired to be hard on ourselves.

Whatever you've done, it's forgivable. God is eager to forgive you—and if he, the Creator and judge of the universe, can forgive you, then you can certainly forgive yourself. Choose to believe today that whatever it is that you have not been able to forgive yourself for can be absolved; choose to believe that you are worth forgiving; and choose to believe that forgiving yourself will ultimately open new levels of success and blessing to you in the future.

1 It's time to set yourself free. What are the offenses, the mistakes, the failures, or the disappointments for which you need to forgive yourself?

_____

_____

_____

_____

_____

_____

_____

_____

_____

_____

_____

2 Throughout *Let It Go* and in this workbook, I've tried to make sure you understand that forgiveness is a choice. It's a decision, not an emotion. Will you choose today to forgive yourself? Circle yes or no.

Yes   No

3 By choosing to forgive yourself, you are taking a giant step forward into the bright future that's ahead of you. Take a moment to record the fact that you have forgiven yourself today (date it, if you'd like), that you are free to enjoy your life and pursue your future as never before, and that you are not going to look back and be held captive by unforgiveness again!

_____

_____

_____

_____

_____

_____

_____

_____

_____

_____

_____

Remember: "Sometimes we are our own worst enemy when it comes to forgiveness" *(Let It Go,* p. 185).

You Are Not Your Actions

You may remember my story about dropping a hot cast-iron skillet on our brand-new carpet when I was a child. Though it made a mark I could never erase, it also taught me a lesson I could never forget: I, as a person, was not defined by my actions.

Accidents happen to all of us. Sometimes they are horrific; sometimes they are less tragic but still have a serious lingering impact. These situations can hijack us emotionally for the rest of our lives if we don't understand that they were external situations that happened, not demonstrations of our internal character or our heart. And as I see it, the way to do that is to recognize the grace of God, receive the love of God, and agree with the forgiveness of God toward us. I like to say that good people sometimes do bad things. God knows we make mistakes, and that's why he looks beyond them to see our motives and intentions. He knows we are not our actions, and we need to believe that too.

1 Have you ever done something that had negative consequences and been called bad for doing it? Circle yes or no.

Yes   No

2 Have you ever had the very best intentions and then had something go wrong or happen accidentally, with a bad result? Circle yes or no.

Yes   No

3 Think about your answers to questions 1 and 2. Was there negative or evil intent in your heart when you did those things? Circle yes or no.

Yes   No

4 Could the things that happened to you have happened just as easily to someone else in the same circumstances at the same time? Circle yes or no.

Yes   No

5 I hope your answers to questions 1–4 will help you separate who you are from what you've done. I'd like to you to copy the words in quotation marks below. Then fill in the blank for "I am not" with things you've been accused of or lies you've believed about yourself. Then, finally, complete the unfinished sentence beginning with "I am." Then keep writing additional thoughts or feelings that follow. Here's the sentence to copy: "Even though I may have done some things that hurt people, those

things do not define who I am. I am not (fill in the blank with words that apply). I am (fill in the blank, and keep going!)"

_____

_____

_____

_____

_____

_____

_____

_____

_____

_____

_____

_____

_____

_____

_____

_____

Remember: "We must reidentify ourselves as to who we are at the core of our being, who God created us to be, not who we are in our worst moments" *(Let It Go,* p. 189).

Better Than the Worst

One of the great lessons I have learned over many years of life and working with people is that we are better than the worst things we do. If there is anything that can convince us that we are so much better than our worst thoughts or actions, it's the love of God. As a pastor, I have preached about this love for years. As I human being, I have lived in it all my life. I can absolutely guarantee you that it's the best thing available on earth. It's mind-blowing in its depth, in its goodness, in its purity, and in its power to make your life awesome.

The love of God cannot be earned because it isn't based on anything you do; it's based on who God is. He loves you because he wants to, even though he knows your deepest, darkest, most shameful secrets—and he never changes his mind about his love for you. One of the amazing things about his love is that he pours it out with full knowledge of everything you've ever done or will do. And he chooses to keep loving you. Your actions simply aren't powerful enough to decrease or cancel his love for you. It isn't about you; it's about how he feels toward you.

1 Think about the worst thing you have ever done. Now write about why you are better than that.

_____

_____

_____

_____

_____

_____

_____

_____

_____

_____

_____

_____

2 Have you ever defined another person by something hurtful or offensive that he or she did? Are you open to revising your opinion about that person, believing that he or she is also better than that one action? Circle yes or no.

Yes   No

3 If there's anything that really may be "too good to be true," it's the love of God. But it is true. Will you choose today to believe that God loves you? Circle yes or no.

Yes   No

4 Take a few moments to write some things that are true about yourself and then follow them with "but God loves me anyway!" For example, you might say something like, "I can be short-tempered when I'm under pressure, but God loves me anyway!"

_____

_____

_____

_____

_____

_____

_____

_____

_____

_____

_____

_____

_____

Remember: "You are better than the worst thing you have ever done. You are not who you once were nor who you will be tomorrow. Your life is a work of art in progress from the Masterpiece Maker of the Universe" *(Let It Go,* p. 193).

Inside Out

I hope you found it as interesting as I did when I shared in *Let It Go* about how the human body heals itself when injury occurs. When your soul has been injured or damaged, healing begins in your mind and in your heart. It comes as you learn to think and feel differently about yourself.

You may have some thoughts about yourself that are deeply embedded in your brain. Some of them, perhaps, didn't even originate with you, but with an angry parent, a jealous sibling, or schoolmate who said you were ugly, stupid, or would never amount to anything. If you believed those false accusations, as many people do, it's time to eradicate them and replace them with thoughts that are true. If you have believed lies about yourself, they've probably led to negative feelings about yourself, so now it's time to let the truth lead you to a place of feeling great about who you are. I believe that you are a tremendous person, full of potential and destined for success. I know that you are worth loving, no matter what you've done. Start to believe these things, and healing will begin to flow from the inside out.

1 In your own words, explain why it's so important for healing to take place from the inside out.

_____

_____

_____

_____

_____

_____

2 What are three specific damaging thoughts you've had about yourself that need to change for healing, strength, and wholeness to come into your life?

_____

_____

_____

_____

_____

_____

_____

_____

3 Look at the three thoughts you wrote in answer to question 2. Now jot down three positive thoughts with which you can replace those.

_____

_____

_____

_____

_____

---

4 Healing from the inside out can take time and energy. Having a support network around you can help immensely. Who are the trustworthy friends, counselors, or people in a recovery group that you'd be willing to have accompany you on your healing journey?

Remember: "Just as our body begins its healing triage reflexively, flushing out our wound and bringing extra nutrients to the injury, so we must wash away the sin that so easily entangles us and bring extraordinary compassion to ourselves. Even if you don't believe you can do it, you must at least attempt to allow God to do it supernaturally" *(Let It Go, p. 195)*.

Write It Off

Today, I'd like to ask you to write or otherwise depict a brief biography about yourself. You may want to write in sentences or paragraphs. Use a list of individual words, or interpret yourself with colors or shapes, or in some other artistic way. Tell the world who you are!

Chapter 12
Uprooted

Before you begin: Please familiarize yourself with Chapter 12 of Let It Go, *pages 199–215.*

Just as a healthy, vibrant garden requires daily weeding to stay beautiful and hearty, the human soul requires vigilance and diligence to keep out weeds of unforgiveness, bitterness, and anger so it can stay healthy and strong too. We must examine our hearts daily to make sure that hurtful words or glances, genuine offenses, and deep wounds don't take root in us in such a way that they rob us of our health, steal our beauty, and bring negativity and ruin to our personalities.

Good gardeners know that breaking off a weed at ground level leaves the most dangerous part of it below the surface of the soil. If it's just picked, and not pulled up by the root, it will only return with a vengeance! Good gardeners also have a few trusty and useful tools at their disposal.

Likewise, you need to understand that the weeds that threaten your soul must be pulled up by their roots from the deep places where they have caused pain, and you have some tools for eliminating the weeds. Two of the most important are acknowledgment and grief.

1 Think about a specific offense or wound you are dealing with now or that has hurt you in the past. *Why* was it so painful? Check all that apply.

_____ I felt disrespected.

_____ I felt ignored.

_____ I felt devalued.

_____ I felt betrayed.

_____ I felt used.

_____ I felt abused.

_____ I felt misunderstood.

_____ I felt abandoned.

_____ I simply felt "wronged."

_____ I felt treated unfairly / I did not deserve what happened.

2 If you would like to elaborate on the feeling(s) you checked above or if you would like to mention some feeling not listed and elaborate on that, use the space below and a separate sheet of paper if needed.

_____

_____

_____

_____

_____

_____

_____

_____

_____

_____

3 Two ways to express grief are to talk about it and to write about it. Would you like to start by writing about a specific wound, loss, or offense in the space below? Begin by naming the encounter or event that has caused you pain, then acknowledge and explain why it hurt. Then, let your feelings (and even your tears) flow. Keep writing on a separate sheet of paper if you need to.

_____

_____

_____

_____

_____

_____

_____

_____

_____

_____

_____

Remember: "It only takes one weed left unchecked to ruin the entire agricultural system for the healthy plants that we want to grow there" *(Let It Go,* p. 201).

Drop the Charges

I have written a good bit in *Let It Go* and in this workbook about the importance of forgiving yourself. I want to dig a little deeper into that issue right now, because sometimes the weeds that grow up in our souls have their roots in unforgiveness toward ourselves, not toward others.

One of the primary situations in which people fail to forgive themselves takes place when they violate their core values, meaning, the principles and ideals they believe to be right, good, and essential to who they are. Core values are the qualities that give people a sense of self-respect and pride. When we can identify our core values, we can see what brings us fulfillment in life (when those values are honored and expressed) and we can also see what offends us and hurts our souls (when those values are violated).

Violating one's own core values seems to be harder to get over than shouting out angry words or doing something accidentally hurtful to someone else. But forgiving ourselves can't be limited to certain actions or behaviors. It must apply as much to offenses against our own values as it does to our other misdeeds.

1 What are some of your core values? Circle all that apply.

Authenticity	Balance	Challenge
Compassion	Courage	Dependability
Discipline	Excellence	Faith
Faithfulness	Family	Fidelity
Frugality	Generosity	Genuineness
Hard work	Honesty	Humility
Independence	Innovation	Integrity
Intellect	Justice	Kindness
Loyalty	Nonviolence	Open communication
Passion	Personal growth	Productivity

Pure-heartedness	Reaching goals	Respect
Responsibility	Risk	Security
Sensitivity	Service	Sincerity
Success	Trust	Trustworthiness
Truth	Understanding	

Other:

_____

_____

2 Think about a situation in which you have really struggled to forgive yourself. Does it involve, on some level, a violation of your core values? Circle yes or no. For example, if you launched a disrespectful verbal assault on someone, you may feel guilty about the words you spoke, but on a deeper level you violated the core value of respect.

Yes   No

3 I urge you right now to forgive yourself for violating your core value(s). Use the space below to declare in writing that you forgive yourself for that violation today!

_____

_____

_____

_____

_____

_____

_____

_____

Remember: "Those who have so violated their own core values that they live in a perpetual state of self-flagellation . . . may punish themselves subconsciously (_Let It Go_, p. 205).

To the Rescue

The problem with weeds in a garden is that they choke the life out of healthy plants and they rob nutrients from flowers or produce. Whether people are trying to grow roses or tomatoes, what they want is the flower or the fruit—the most beautiful flower or the most perfect fruit possible, not some half-wilted, spotty specimen that has lost its value because a weed stole its nutrients!

The same thing happens when weeds of punishing yourself long after an incident is resolved overtake your soul. Those things keep you from experiencing the vitality and success you're destined for. So what do you do to set yourself free and ensure that nothing stands between you and the bright future that's yours for the taking? I have three suggestions: Admit it, convert it, and close it. You can read more about what each of these means on pages 213–215 of _Let It Go_, and I encourage you to do so right now.

1 When I write in *Let It Go* about admitting what we've done wrong, I mention that I am a great believer in having close friends in whom you can confide your victories and your defeats, your good moves and your not-so-good moves. To whom can you admit and talk about a wound or offense you've caused?

_____

_____

_____

_____

2 How can you convert your pain from something that affects you negatively to a force that can influence others in positive ways? For example, you could write about it, teach a class, have coffee with someone who's going through a similar experience, or, if you're artistic, you could create an inspiring painting or work of art to depict the conversion. List some ways you can convert your pain.

_____

_____

_____

_____

_____

_____

_____

_____

_____

_____

_____

3 Some people bring closure to an offense by writing it on a piece of paper and burning it in a safe way. Some bury a symbol of the offense in the ground. Some don't need any physical action at all; they just make a decision to close that chapter of their lives and move on. How will you bring closure to something for which you have been punishing yourself?

_____

_____

_____

_____

_____

_____

_____

Remember: "In this life we will never know the perfect beauty of the Garden of Eden. But we can know what it's like to weed out the bitter roots that threaten our peace and well-being. We can let go of the blame we place on ourselves and move to a new place of freedom and fruit-bearing productivity" (*Let It Go,* p. 215).

Write It Off

I invite you today to think about your soul as a garden. Using words or some other artistic expression, depict the beauty of your soul—including the ways you would feel, the relationships you would cultivate, the goals you would reach, and the things you would enjoy in life—if you were to be diligent every day to keep your soul weed-free.

Chapter 13
Physician, Heal Thyself

Before you begin: Please familiarize yourself with Chapter 13 of Let It Go, *pages 217–232.*

As a pastor, I believe the church should be a community of God's people who may have struggled and suffered, but who have also been healed by his grace and are now equipped and eager to help others. Unfortunately, that's not always the case. Too often, churches are filled with wounded people seeking help they do not get for various reasons, and these wounded people, out of their own pain, can make the wounds of others worse instead of better.

While I honestly acknowledge the sad state of the church today, I also remain optimistic and prayerful that this institution will be healed, so it can arise to be the bright light of hope and truth, the place of peace, and the instrument of healing, wholeness, and victory that God intends it to be.

I hope you have had positive experiences in churches and that every time you've sought help, support, healing, or encouragement among God's people, you have found it. I've also talked to enough people and observed enough situations to know that many people have not had uplifting, strengthening encounters with the church. Some people haven't even had neutral experiences; their interactions with church people have been negative or even hurtful—completely the opposite of an organization designed to represent God's goodness and love!

1 I know it could be painful, but would you write in the space below what your experiences with churches and church people have been?

_____

_____

_____

_____

_____

_____

_____

_____

_____

2 Complete this sentence by checking all that apply. I believe churches and/or people who go to church are:

_____ condescending

_____ exclusive

_____ harsh

_____ hypocritical

_____ inclusive and welcoming

_____ intimidating

_____ insincere

_____ judgmental

_____ kind

_____ loving

_____ merciful

_____ narrow-minded

_____ open-minded

_____ patient

_____ people of substance who really have something to offer

_____ safe

_____ skeptical of people who seem to have problems

_____ superficial

_____ supportive

_____ well-meaning

3 In your own words, what kind of place do you think the church should be if it is to reflect God's loving character and gracious nature?

_____

_____

_____

_____

_____

_____

_____

_____

_____

Remember: "The church should be a place of healing and restoration, a bright reflection of the mercy, grace, and love of our Father God" *(Let It Go,* p. 223).

Three in One

When people talk about being hurt or disappointed by "the church," they don't mean a sleek contemporary concrete-and-glass structure that holds thousands of worshippers on a Sunday morning, nor do they mean a traditional brick building with stained-glass windows or a steeple. The building doesn't have any affect on them; it's the people inside who can do so much damage. The trouble comes from several different places: church leadership, church membership, and the way the churches and church people as a whole present themselves to the world. You can read at length about these three aspects of the church on pages 222–231 of *Let It Go*; I encourage you to do that right now and then consider the questions below.

1 Have you ever been hurt, disappointed, misled, or abused by someone in a church leadership position? Would you acknowledge that and begin to release the pain by writing about it in the space provided?

_____

_____

_____

_____

_____

_____

_____

_____

_____

_____

_____

_____

_____

2 Of all people who should never have hurt you, church leaders are at the top of the list. Will you choose today to forgive the one who did damage to you? Circle yes or no.

Yes   No

3 If you agree to forgive a church leader who hurt you, you are taking a giant step forward in healing and wholeness. Write your declaration of forgiveness below:

_____

_____

_____

_____

_____

_____

4 Have you ever been disappointed, rejected, betrayed, used, or hurt in any way by a member or group of members in a church? Would you acknowledge that and release the pain of that situation by describing in the space below what happened and how you felt?

_____

_____

_____

_____

_____

_____

_____

_____

_____

_____

_____

_____

5 Church members should not hurt people; they should love them. Will you choose today to forgive those who wounded you? Circle yes or no.

Yes   No

6 If you agree to forgive the church member(s) who hurt you, you are making a huge move in the right direction. Write your declaration of forgiveness below:

_____

_____

_____

_____

_____

_____

_____

7 How would you say the world in general views the church at large? How do you think the church presents itself to the world?

_____

_____

_____

_____

_____

_____

_____

_____

_____

_____

_____

_____

Remember: "I believe the problems in the Christian church here in the first rays of our twenty-first-century dawn emerge from the convergence of three areas—church leadership, church membership, and the church's relationship to the world at large" *(Let It Go,* pp. 223–224).

Emergency Care

I believe the church has the greatest potential of any organization ever known to bring help and healing to people in life-changing ways.

I hope that we have seen the church at its worst and that things will only get better from now on. I pray that the church will become a place of compassion and mercy, of understanding and forgiveness, of truth and freedom. I pray it will become a place where wounded people feel welcome, loved, supported, and helped as they become part of a community that facilitates healing and strength.

I'm going to do my part to see this happen; and I hope you'll do yours too. We have our work cut out for us, but if enough people commit to the challenge, the most awesome things can happen!

1 Scripture refers to the church as the "Bride of Christ." Knowing Scripture and knowing Christ's loving nature and what kind of bride he desires, what qualities should the church display?

_____

_____

_____

_____

_____

_____

_____

_____

_____

_____

2 The Bible refers to the church as "the Body of Christ." What are some of the characteristics of Jesus Christ that you most want to experience in the context of a church?

_____

_____

_____

_____

_____

_____

_____

_____

_____

_____

_____

Remember: "We must reclaim [the church] as the Body of Christ, a community of the forgiven administering compassion, healing, and grace to others in need" *(Let It Go,* p. 232).

Write It Off

Let me encourage you to dream a little. Using words or some other creative way of expressing yourself, depict what kind of place you wish the church would be and what your best hopes are for wounded people who seek help in the church. Then, rather than imposing your desires on the church and judging a church for not being what you want or need, *work and pray to become* what you've described. Individuals who demonstrate the positive potential of the church are the only way the church will ever change!

Chapter 14
Available for What's Next

Before you begin: Please familiarize yourself with Chapter 14 of Let It Go, *pages 233–246.*

I write in *Let It Go:* "Forgiveness caps the leak in your own energy and enables you to stop the damage it causes you, minimize the peripheral damage it causes others, and ultimately restore to you the infusion of energy denied to your dreams by the emotionally and physically draining leak from your human soul" (p. 237).

One of the best reasons to forgive is to sever your ties with past situations and relationships so you can move forward into your future and go after those things you've always dreamed of. Once you've done the work of forgiveness, you are free to joyfully anticipate and embrace your future; you are truly available for what's next!

1 Now that you've almost reached the end of this workbook, what are some of the things from which you truly feel released, healed, and set free as a result of choosing to forgive?

_____

_____

_____

_____

_____

_____

2 Jot down the first few ideas that come to mind when you think about what's next for you. What do you want to be and do?

_____

_____

_____

_____

_____

_____

_____

Remember: "Simply put, it's about turning your head around from looking behind you, realizing where you are right now, and then looking forward to your future" *(Let It Go,* p. 233).

New Investments

Once you truly let some things go, you may be surprised to realize how much more energy and time you have. When you're no longer giving your attention and emotions to the negative situations that once commandeered it, you have a lot of positive energy for other things.

That's exciting to think about, and I would offer a word of caution as you consider it: You can let go of old wounds and offenses, but they won't let go of you quite so easily. When you fall back into old emotions and ways of dealing with things, simply catch yourself, stop it, and decide right then to put your thoughts and energy into new, positive situations.

I believe great opportunities are waiting for you just around the corner. Your mind has been freed from past thoughts and it can dream again. Your heart has been healed from past pain, and it can hope again. The blinders have come off of your inner vision, and you can see. With these abilities to dream again, hope again, and see clearly again, you'll find out where to put your new energy and attention.

1 Do you believe, as I do, that something great awaits you? Circle yes or no.

Yes   No

2 When you fall back into an old, negative emotional pattern, how will you get yourself out of it?

_____

_____

_____

_____

_____

3 How will you prepare yourself to embrace new opportunities? Think in terms of preparing yourself both mentally and physically.

_____

_____

_____

_____

_____

Remember: "I challenge you to begin to plan for the new energy and efforts you have saved to be redirected to something more deserving of your time" (*Let It Go*, p. 237).

Lifting Weights

When you've been through a time of struggling with unforgiveness, anger, and resentment, you pour your energy into those things as an athlete pours energy into training. But athletes don't only train in the fine points of their chosen sports: They also cross-train, developing strength in ways they may never use on a field or a court, but that exercise vital muscles needed to excel in their areas of expertise.

When you practice forgiveness, you still have the strengths developed before you forgave. You may have "muscles" of standing up for yourself, compassion for others, wisdom, or a new level of patience and emotional strength. Use those muscles as athletes use cross-training and put them to work doing what you love and what you were created to do.

When the burden of your past is lifted, things that once seemed impossible no longer seem so daunting. You begin to feel as though you can do what you're made to do and go after your dreams—and capture them and live them.

1 What emotional muscles did you develop in the past season?

_____

_____

_____

_____

_____

_____

_____

2 How can your emotional muscles and strength serve you well as you use them to pursue new opportunities and enjoy life in new ways?

_____

_____

_____

_____

_____

_____

Remember: "When we practice forgiveness, we use the muscles we have been forced to develop to return to what should have been our primary focus all along" *(Let It Go,* p. 238).

Brotherly Love

In *Let It Go,* I share some insights into the biblical account of the prodigal son. You can reread it on pages 239–241. The key lesson we need to learn from this story is that we can waste our lives comparing ourselves with others, *especially* when they seem blessed and we feel ignored. Or, we can refuse to be bitter and resentful—and join the party! We must keep moving forward and stay focused on the great opportunities and the bright future ahead of us. When someone else receives a blessing, even if you feel it's unfair, set your gaze on the good things in your life, rejoice with that person (or at least enjoy the celebration) and know that tremendous things are on the way for you!

1 Has there ever been a situation in which you could have been celebrating but chose to be angry or jealous instead? What was it and what did you learn from it?

_____

_____

_____

_____

_____

_____

_____

_____

_____

_____

_____

_____

2 What are some of the dangers of comparing your life to someone else's? What might you miss while you are busy focusing on another person's blessings?

_____

_____

_____

_____

_____

_____

_____

Remember: "If we are to be available for what's next, the next blessing, the next gift from God, the next amazing opportunity, then we must not compare our journey to anyone else's" *(Let It Go,* p. 241).

True Grit

You have been through a lot! Like a grain of sand that embeds itself in an oyster, irritating its soft inside until a beautiful pearl emerges, the pain and problems you have suffered have created something beautiful in you. It may be the discovery of new strength and wisdom or the revival of an old dream you thought had died. Know this: It cost you something to become who you are today. Treasure the lessons; put them together like pearls on a string to make something of value you can share with the world!

1 What has it cost you to become who you are?

_____

_____

_____

_____

_____

2 I don't believe your destiny is connected to what you lose, but to what remains in your life, even if something has come from a place of pain or irritation. What remains for you? What is in your life now that can be valuable to you and others?

_____

_____

_____

_____

_____

_____

Remember: "Dive for your pearls like a treasure hunter searching the ocean floor, discovering the beautiful gift that's waiting inside the grit" *(Let It Go,* p. 242).

Commencement Exercise

A commencement, or graduation, is a time to celebrate! And now that you have dealt with so much bitterness and pain, you have graduated to a new level of peace, freedom, and maturity and to a time to view your future through the lens of possibility and promise!

But you didn't reach this place alone. Just as graduates from schools and universities invite friends, family, and others who have helped them reach this milestone to observe and celebrate their commencement, why don't you take time to appreciate those who have walked with you and assisted you through some hard times?